FLY FISHING THE TIDEWATERS

CONTENTS

ACKNOWLEDGMENTS

There is a time to fish and a time to write. At the time this book is going to press, I am in my fiftieth year, and my wife, Dana Jennings, and I have just had our second child, Rachel. Her brother, Izaak, is three years old. Because of "the Izaak years," I have had less time to fish but much more time to reflect. Thanks to Izaak and Rachel for causing me to slow down, and to write. The most thanks goes to my loving wife and best friend, Dana, for encouragement, for putting up with my "layers" of fishing and photography equipment, and for supporting, and joining in, my passion for fly fishing.

So much I owe to my parents, Ruth and Irwin Earnhardt, who are no longer with me. They gave me the opportunity to explore from my earliest years. Dad gave me my first fly rod at six and fly-tying vise on my ninth birthday, a Herter's "Number 9." Mom and Dad took equal time nurturing my love for fishing.

Special thanks goes to fishing friends and mentors who have enriched my life: Joel Arrington, who taught me much about fishing but even more about lying to companions holding fish by saying, "Just one more picture"; Captain Nat Ragland (Marathon, Florida), who was as good a guide on days we didn't fish as he was on the flats; Buzz Bryson, a self-described tackle "nerd," but the best of fishing companions and a fountain of information; Mark Morris, another barrister who knows that fishing is God's reward for good lawyers; and Robert Bryant, a wonderful fishing friend and the best fly fisherman I know who doesn't tie his own flies.

Thanks also goes to my friends at a very special place, Harkers Island, North Carolina, where there are no entry gates and no big houses, but a love of the sea and all that it brings. Donald Willis, Paul Hodges, Bob and Rob Pasfield, and Captain Tommy Gunn are just a few of the special people on this special island.

In recent years much of the fly fishing I have done would not have been possible without the help of Donnie and Rob Jones of Jones Brothers Marine in Morehead City, who let me use and test any number of their excellent boats. Thanks also goes to the Jones brothers for letting me live out my fantasy as a boat designer by allowing me to tinker with various fly-fishing designs.

Fly fishing is a sport where there are no strangers, just new friends. To list the number of people who have been helpful in the preparation of this book would require more space than my publisher could afford. At the risk of leaving out some, I will, not in alphabetical order, list friends, some whom I have not met in person, who provided support, pictures, information, and flies: Peter Van Gytenbeek, who gave me a slot on the masthead of Fly Fishing in Saltwaters; Bob Popovics, "Mr. Epoxy," who gives new meaning to fly-fishing enthusiasm; Flip Pallot, who gave me the opportunity to work with his excellent program the "Walker's Cay Chronicles"; Dan Blanton, a photographer and California angler without equal; Franc White, the "Southern Sportsman," a longtime fishing friend and traveling companion; Jim Dean, my first editor at Wildlife in North Carolina and great fishing companion; Captain Bill Harris, a pioneering fly-rod skipper on the southern Outer Banks; Jim Brown, the best speckled-trout fisherman I know; Bill Anderson, a walking encyclopedia of the Chesapeake Bay; Richmond anglers Ronnie and Glenn Sides for photographs and information on the history of the Chesapeake fishery; Captain Norman Miller, a fabulous fisherman, who had the left side of his brain replaced with that of a large red drum; Steve Wilson, a great photographer and fishing companion; Captains Mike Able and Jerry Ciandella, who provided pictures, information, and flies for the Georgia / South Carolina fishery; Captains Jon Cave and Dennis Hammond for their help in understanding Florida's Indian River; Captain Mike Kenfield, who provided pictures and information on northeastern waters from Connecticut to Cape Cod; Ed Jaworowski, a fabulous caster, writer, and photographer, who provided much valuable information; Captain Bubby Rodriguez, a pioneering fly fisherman in Louisiana marshes and surrounding Gulf waters; and finally, Stanley Windborne, a great angler and one of those rare people who can make blowing wind, cold temperatures, and no fish a happy occasion.

To Trout Unlimited, and the Board of Directors on which I served, for allowing me to chair the International Committee. In that position I saw the sheer joy that fly fishing brought anglers in Russia, China, Yugoslavia, and other countries. Through TU I met some of my most cherished friends in the Murmansk Big Fish Club, Murmansk, Russia.

Thanks to Gladys Carney, whose friendship, typing skills, mastery of the English language, attention to detail, and unceasing support have made this book, and every other worthwhile thing I have written since law school, possible. Also, thanks to Tara Melton-Miller and Mary Tudor for their help in preparing this manuscript. Their word-processing skills, sense of humor, and willingness to always fit me into their schedules kept me sane. "Just one more little change . . ."

A special thanks to Nick Lyons, publisher, gentle mentor, and friend, who gave me the confidence to believe that this book was possible. Thanks also goes to David Williams and Duane Raver, both great artists, who lent their time and talent to the preparation of this book.

Finally, to Lefty Kreh, who has been an inspiration and source of constant innovation for several generations of fly fishermen and fishing writers. "Forever thirty-nine," Lefty's energy and enthusiasm have never ceased to amaze me. More than any other fishing companion, he has been a fountain of support with a note, the hottest fly, or the worst joke. From New Zealand to the Outer Banks, trips with him have been graduate courses in casting, presentation, and how to avoid gourmet food. Thanks, Lefty!

FOREWORD

There are many people who write "how to" books on fishing. In my judgment perhaps 20 percent of them are written from actual experience. Most books are constructed from the writer's interviews and with a minimal experience in the subject. At this moment I see publications by trout-fishing writers who have suddenly discovered saltwater fly fishing and are writing about it—from limited experience. Every now and then someone who has really lived, observed, and studied a subject writes a book. One example of this is Tom Earnhardt's *Fly Fishing the Tidewaters*.

I first met Tom in 1972 at a Saltwater Fly Rodders of America convention on the Outer Banks of North Carolina. There was a break in convention activities. Grabbing my fly rod and camera, I proceeded to the beach, which at times can offer some of the most exciting surf fishing in North America. A storm had passed not long before, and the waves were a bit rough and crashing the shore. Standing hip-deep in the waves and occasionally getting drenched by one was a fly fisherman who was throwing his offering into the roiled waters. He didn't catch anything while I watched, but several things were evident. First, he could cast—even under those conditions. Second, here was a guy who loved saltwater fly fishing, no matter what the elements offered. I took some pictures of Tom and we soon became friends. Tom has a 220-volt body and lives in a 100-volt world. He is constantly in motion and is one of the best saltwater fly fishermen I have known—around the world.

Not only has he spent years prowling the inshore and offshore waters of North Carolina, he has tested many other waters, too. He has fished for years with many of the best guides in the Keys. Believe me, giant tarpon, bonefish, and any damn thing Tom can throw a fly at is no stranger to him.

He has helped me teach classes on fly casting, is a superb photographer, and has written articles on fly fishing over the years. He loves to teach and he is a great fishing companion.

There are few people who know more about fishing the tidewaters. I don't care where you live, in the U.S. or in other countries, if you fish the inshore waters, this book will help you. It is not a book to read casually; it must be studied. As your skills progress in fly fishing, go back to the book again and again—you'll learn even more.

This book has been written by a fly fisherman who has the experience and credentials. Welcome to *Fly Fishing the Tidewaters*.

—Lefty Kreh

INTRODUCTION

The growth of fly fishing in salt water is nothing short of a quiet revolution in angling. Old refrigerators filled with squid are being moved out of many tackle shops to make room for Deceivers, Clousers, and Candies—names unknown to most anglers even a few years ago. People rigging fly tackle are now a relatively common sight at beaches and marinas, while only a few years ago fly fishers would have been as rare as woolly mammoths. Although warm-water destinations still get most of the press, the tidewaters near some of the nation's largest population centers are where much of the growth in fly fishing is occurring.

From New England to Cape Canaveral and along the Gulf Coast, the main reason for the bounty awaiting fly rodders is the presence of great tidal estuaries. At the heart of each estuary is spartina (cordgrass), which holds barrier islands together, acts as a buffer against great storms, pulls nutrients out of the water, serves as a breeding ground and nursery area for all manner of gamefish and their prey, and is itself part of the beginning of the food web. Roughly 90 percent of all commercial and sport fish along the East and Gulf coasts, both inshore and offshore, owe their existence to these spartina-rimmed estuaries.

The largest and most significant estuarine systems are the Chesapeake Bay, the Pamlico/Albemarle sounds of North Carolina, and the vast Delta region of Louisiana. Smaller but no less important in the scheme of things are the estuaries of the Jersey shore, the Delaware Bay, and the eastern shores of Maryland and Virginia. Among the most productive and beautiful estuarine systems are the marshes and creeks behind the barrier islands of South Carolina and Georgia, which are accentuated by six- to ten-foot tides. The spartina marshes merge with mangroves and come to an end in Florida's magnificent Indian River estuary. Finally, even when you exclude Louisiana's Delta lands, the Gulf Coast is still blessed with extensive tidelands from Florida to the Mexican border.

For fly fishermen there is a large variety of fish species, especially on the East Coast. This abundance is partly the yield of productive estuaries, and also the result of the meeting of cold and warm water. Off the capes of Virginia and the Carolinas, fish from the cool waters of the Mid-Atlantic Bight meet the tropicals of the South Atlantic Bight. Thus, at the mouth of the Chesapeake Bay, for example, anglers can chase stripers, false albacore, bluefish, bonito, red and black drum, common and spotted weakfish, tautog, and cobia. Just offshore there are dolphin, yellowfin tuna, amberjack, and all of the Atlantic billfish. Because of the differing temperature tolerances of various species, there is an array of gamefish for fly fishermen along much of the East and Gulf coasts almost year-round.

Although I have fished with the fly rod in salt water for almost thirty years, only in the last decade have I come to appreciate the unique opportunities available to fly fishers in my home waters. There is certainly no dearth of anglers fishing with all other types of tackle in the waters of the East and Gulf coasts. However, I—and others before me—have discovered that fly tackle is not only the most exciting way to catch fish, but also one of the most efficient. For many years the fish I caught in the waters of North Carolina and the adjoining states were, in my mind, mere appetizers for the main course: the fish of the Florida Keys. Throughout the seventies and early eighties I was like the Prodigal Son as I left home to seek bonefish, tarpon, and permit one thousand miles to the south. I still love fishing the tropics, but most of my fishing time and energy is now spent on the waters nearest my home.

Early on, when I was discussing the scope of this book with fly-fishing friends, some thought I had chosen a title that seemed limiting. On the contrary, the term "tidewaters" is all-encompassing. The fact is that most fly fishing is done in tidewaters—coastal rivers, bays, sounds, the surf, and even nearshore and offshore waters that are often overlooked as places influenced by the tide. Most of us are used to fishing in areas where the rise and fall of the tide is easily discernible. We can sense the influence of the tide when we see a buoy leaning landward or seaward, when we see water rising or falling next to a jetty or a bridge, or when we feel the incoming tide while standing in the surf. Several miles up a coastal river or out to sea, tidal changes may not be so evident, but they are just as significant.

Fly fishing is my preferred method for taking most gamefish, but over the years I have continued to use and enjoy other tackle and fishing techniques. It is my hope that this book will help the sport of saltwater fly fishing become more approachable for many anglers who may have stayed away for the wrong reasons. For many of my best fishing friends, fly fishing is not the primary method of taking fish in salt water, but it is an integral part of their arsenal. Fly fishing in salt water is not always easy—it can be as simple or as complex a sport as you want to make it—but no other method of catching fish is more enjoyable. Like home cooking or food from a five-star restaurant, fly fishing in salt water is always satisfying.

Whether you live in San Francisco, Norfolk, or New Orleans, this book is about your waters. It is about opening people's minds to angling opportunities that have long been closed by self-imposed limitations rather than by fishing regulations. In exploring these opportunities I have tried not to "reinvent the wheel," rehashing materials on knots, casting, and fly patterns already well covered in other books. I have, however, attempted to provide ample "how to" information so that any angler can enter the brave new world of saltwater fly fishing with confidence.

When compared with other sportfishing techniques, saltwater fly fishing in most areas is still in its infancy. Over the next decade the area from New York to north Florida, much of the Gulf Coast, and much of this country's Pacific coastline will see significant growth and innovation in fly fishing. Welcome to angling's quiet revolution.

PART I

SALTWATER FLY FISHING
A Sport for All Coastal Waters

CHAPTER 1

BREAKING OLD HABITS AND CONFRONTING MYTHS

On a beautiful June day in the early 1980s I noticed a push of water caused by several large cobia swimming near a buoy at Cape Lookout on the southern end of North Carolina's Outer Banks. The tide was dead low and the buoy stood straight, indicating there was no current and that the flood tide had not started. As is their habit, the cobia were swimming in a counterclockwise orbit around the buoy. The fish seemed unhurried, and occasionally a dorsal or the tip of a tail would appear as the wide chocolate-brown fish continued their circling game.

I reached into my live well, pulled out a half-pound croaker, and impaled it on a 7/0 hook. I stood on the bow of my boat trying to pick out the largest of the herd. There were a half-dozen fish, and they all appeared to be between thirty and fifty pounds. I had been in that position a number of times and knew the routine well. I was trying to pick out the largest fish so that I could lob the croaker in front of it. Suddenly it occurred to me that there were several fly rods in the boat, including one for a 12-weight line, and a couple boxes of streamers. I had just returned from a week's trip of fly rodding for tarpon at Homasassa on Florida's Gulf Coast. At that point in my angling life I had already caught many large tarpon on a fly, and numerous other species of fish on the East Coast, including cobia. Why, then, I thought, was I lobbing a live bait with a heavy spinning rod to a cobia in near-perfect fly-fishing conditions? The answer was simple: That was the way I had *always* fished for cobia around buoys.

Old habits die hard, and it's easy to get into ruts—especially fishing ruts. That June day proved to be an important one in my angling evolution. I quickly rigged a five-inch-long green-and-white Deceiver with a short piece of eighty-pound shock tippet. With a system 12 rod I laid the Deceiver beside what appeared to be the largest fish in the school. There was really no surprise when the fish turned and inhaled the large fly. Less than a half hour later the fish, between forty and fifty pounds, was at boat side, and the fly was clearly visible on the right side of its mouth. I released the cobia unharmed but returned to the marina a changed person.

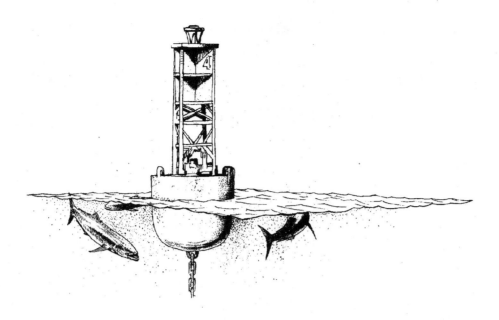

As is their habit, the cobia were swimming in a counterclockwise orbit around the buoy.

Large fish on any tackle excite me. That cobia, however, more than any fish, helped to change the way I looked at the coastal waters of North Carolina and at the waters of surrounding states to the north and south. Even though fly tackle had been part of my saltwater arsenal since the late sixties, I was suddenly struck by the fact that most of my saltwater fly-fishing friends and I knew far more about fisheries a thousand miles away than we did about our home shores. Like many early fly rodders in North Carolina and those of other states living near salt water, I did not regard the waters of my region as "serious fly-fishing waters." Real fly fishermen went to the Florida Keys, the Bahamas, or Central America. Bonefish, tarpon, snook, and permit were, in my mind, the most significant trophies in the fly-fishing universe.

There was no question that on my trips to the tropics I learned a lot about fly-fishing skills from talented Keys guides, such as Captain Nat Ragland, John Emery, Dale Perez, Jose Wejebe, and others. From them I learned speed casting, knots, innovative patterns, and how to "see" and fight fish. Because of its early concentration of fly-fishing talent, the Keys were both the incubator and research-and-development office of saltwater fly fishing.

Today a large number of serious fly rodders still spend their time and money going after the great flats fish and other warm-water prizes of the Keys, Bahamas, and Central America. Much more recently, saltwater fly fishing has expanded to Africa, South America, the north coast of Australia, and to tiny islands in the Pacific. There has been a significant increase in fly rodders in most coastal areas, but I daresay that in the early 1990s more people boarded jets to fish Christmas Island (south of Hawaii) for bonefish than all those who fly fished on the Outer Banks of North Carolina during the same period for all species.

REMOVING MYTH

For many years saltwater fly fishing was surrounded by a fog of myth and mystique. It was a "bigger than life" sport, and there weren't a lot of believers. A fly rod, after all, was designed for trout, bass, and panfish. In most coastal regions people who fished in the ocean used stiff surf sticks or heavy trolling rods for big fish. Only in the last decade, have captains of charter-boat fleets in Virginia and the Carolinas quit using fifty-pound-test line to pursue king mackerel. Again, old habits die hard.

Because most anglers, myself included, had such a limited view of fly tackle and its application, it was difficult not to attribute supernatural skills to those who used fly tackle in salt water. It was easy to believe that only a Joe Brooks, Lefty Kreh, Stu Apt, Lee Wulff, or Ted Williams was capable of catching fish from another dimension on a fly. However, these were among the sport's pioneers who tried to take the myth out of saltwater fly fishing.

Clothed in ignorance, many also assumed that fish that would take flies lived only in the gin-clear water of the tropics. The big three—tarpon, bonefish, and permit—have long been accorded special, even mythical, status. In other waters, however, most gamefish did not get the appreciation and respect accorded their flats cousins. Any fisherman over forty can remember pictures of proud anglers standing beside a pile of large red drum or posing with dozens of giant bluefish on a hanging board. Fortunately, the "gaff'um and club'um" mentality is rapidly disappearing. There are catch limits on many fish, but more important, there seems to be a genuine appreciation for the sporting qualities of most fish. In many areas fly fishermen are leading the way. Bluefish are now treated with respect, and false albacore, a trash fish to some only a few years ago, are now regarded as important sport fish. Even less spectacular fighters, like sea trout, are considered to be worthy adversaries.

The late Joe Brooks was the first angler/writer to make the use of fly tackle in salt water a realistic option for a skeptical angling world.
Photograph by Lefty Kreh

THE SPREADING OF KNOWLEDGE

As fly fishing has blossomed in most coastal areas of this country, it is important for new anglers to realize that there has always been cross-pollination in the sport. Even when the Keys fishery got most of the press, many of the fly patterns and techniques used there had been developed in other parts of the country. Because anglers fished the Keys and then returned home, the new ideas were spread. The great Joe Brooks had home ties and angling ties to both Richmond and Baltimore. Many of the flies that Brooks popularized in his writings came from Maryland angler Tom Loving and Bill Gallasch of Richmond. It was Brooks who helped Lefty Kreh begin his career as an outdoor writer and as the preeminent fly fisherman of his time. In the late fifties Kreh developed his Deceiver pattern in the striped bass waters of the Chesapeake near Crisfield, Maryland. There was a hotbed of fly-fishing interest along the Jersey shore during this period, and it was at Cape May Courthouse at the office of the Saltwater Fly Rodders of America where the first fly-rod world records were kept. When Lefty Kreh left Maryland to run the Miami Metropolitan Fishing Tournament in the late sixties and early seventies, he, like Joe Brooks before him, took knowledge and fly patterns of the Mid-Atlantic to the Keys.

From the West Coast there was also cross-pollination. Writer Jules Cuenin caught stripers on fly tackle in San Francisco Bay as early as 1925. Artist Russ Chatham was, in the fifties and sixties, one of California's best saltwater fly fishermen before moving to Montana. Dan Blanton, one of the country's premiere anglers, developed many of his early patterns, including his Whistlers, in the striped-bass haunts of San Francisco Bay in the 1960s. Blanton and Nick Curcione were among the pioneers of the shooting head and sinking line for Pacific critters. Blanton also fished the Keys but was more important in the development of fisheries in Costa Rica and other Central American countries.

Bill Gallasch of Richmond, Virginia, was one of the first great tiers to begin creating flies for inshore and offshore species.
Photograph by Glen Sides

Lefty Kreh created his famous Deceiver pattern for Chesapeake Bay stripers in the late fifties and has since that time become the acknowledged grand master of saltwater fly fishing in salt waters around the world.
Photograph by Lefty Kreh

Bob Popovics is one of the best-known northeastern anglers, whose epoxy and silicone creations have helped to revo-lutionize saltwater fly tying.
Photograph by Tom Earnhardt

     Many of the surf-fishing and deepwater techniques now used in fly fishing were developed in the Northeast. Nelson Bryant, long-respected outdoor columnist for *The New York Times*, was one of a number of early fly rodders in the region who took stripers, bluefish, bonito, albacore, and weakfish from Cape Cod to Nantucket. It was in the Northeast that nighttime techniques for fly fishing were perfected.

     From the early eighties to the present, no area of the country has had a monopoly on innovation. In the Northeast, Lou Tabory has developed many new patterns and has done much to spread the knowledge of the region. Few casters are better than Philadelphia writer-angler Ed Jaworowski. In New Jersey the godfather of fly fishing is Bob Popovics, the acknowledged master of five-minute epoxy and creator of numerous flies used worldwide. One of the most unlikely superstars in the fly-fishing pantheon is Bob Clouser, a Susquehanna River smallmouth guide who created the Clouser Sinking Minnow. Since the mid-eighties no fly has caught more species of fish from the tropics to the arctic than the Clouser Minnow.

On down the coast, Joel Arrington helped to open up the waters of the Carolinas to fly fishing. This writer and photographer brought Chico Fernandez to North Carolina in 1981 to catch giant channel bass and white marlin on a fly. Arrington was also one of the first to use fly tackle for many other fish in the region, both inshore and offshore.

From Georgetown, South Carolina, to Savannah, Georgia, there is a unique fishery around the semitropical barrier islands of the region, where tide changes can average five to ten feet. Captains Mike Able of Charleston and Fuzzy Davis of Hilton Head have been among the leaders in promoting an almost year-round inshore fishery for red drum on a fly.

In the waters where cordgrass stops and the mangroves start in Florida's Indian River, there is a talented group of guides and a varied fishery. The premier fish of the region would have to be redfish and "gator" spotted

Captain Mike Able has done more than any other angler to introduce fly fishing to the inland waters of South Carolina and Georgia.
Photograph by Captain Jerry Ciandella

weakfish, although ladyfish, tarpon, jack, and snook are also available. Captain Jon Cave is a fisheries biologist, guide, and one of the most innovative fly tiers in the region.

From the Florida Panhandle to south Texas the number of fly fishermen has literally exploded in recent years. Although there is good inshore and offshore fishing, the comeback of the redfish is the main reason for fly rodding's popularity. Although there are excellent guides all along the Gulf, one of the more interesting fisheries has to be the great redfishing in super-shallow water less than an hour from downtown New Orleans. One of the innovators in the region, Captain Bubby Rodriguez, and his partners use unique shallow-draft boats and fly patterns to catch French-speaking redfish.

Fly fishermen in salt water are still a small minority in the fishing world. Wherever you live, on the East, Gulf, or West Coast, the barriers have been broken. Virtually every species of gamefish is sought by fly rodders. Fly fishing in salt water should no longer be considered a sport of the strong, well coordinated, and wealthy. Even if you don't have the resources to hop a plane for some tropical destination, you will find a world of satisfaction and excitement if you are willing to explore the jetties, pilings, surf, and open waters of the shore nearest you. Old habits die hard. . . .

CHAPTER 2

CARRY A FUN ROD

My father was not a pioneer in saltwater fly fishing. In fact, to my knowledge he never caught a fish on a fly in salt water. He was a whiz at fishing with spring lizards (salamanders), crayfish, night crawlers, and every artificial lure imaginable. He owned a couple of fly rods, but most fly-fishing time was devoted to bluegill, bass, and trout. The closest he ever came to fly fishing in salt water was on trips to the Santee-Cooper Reservoir in South Carolina, where he caught "schoolie," landlocked striped bass, on a fly in the mid-sixties. It was about that time that I started carrying a heavy glass fly rod on our trips to the coast. That rod didn't see much action, largely because other angling techniques suited me just fine. I also had a little understanding of how to cast efficiently in windy conditions.

By 1969 I had caught small bluefish in the surf and a few stripers in the Albemarle Sound region of North Carolina. Even though I was in law school at the time, I still managed to slip away on weekends. In October of 1969 I received an invitation to fish with Joel Arrington, who at the time worked for the state of North Carolina as a promoter of inland and coastal fisheries. Joel had invited me to fish with him in Pamlico Sound for large red drum before they headed out to the Ocracoke and Hatteras inlets in late October. On a Friday afternoon we launched Arrington's boat at the little town of Vandameer, North Carolina, on the mainland side of Pamlico Sound. The boat was filled with heavy surf rods, bait, camping equipment, food, Joel's cameras, and my fly rod. Things went fine for the first fifteen miles when, without warning, the motor heaved, choked, and made a loud rattling sound as it died. When the smoke cleared, we looked at the remains of a blown power head. We had no radio, but we were fortunate enough to be near a small marsh island at the mouth of the Neuse River. After a few minutes of paddling and drifting we grounded Arrington's seventeen-foot tri-hull on the small marsh island.

Little did we know that it would be three days before another boat would pass the small island and tow us back to the mainland. At first light the next morning we used our heavy surf tackle and bait to search for red drum around the small marsh island, but there were no takers. At the east end of the island there was an oyster bar extending perhaps fifty feet. The first cast with a MirrOlure on spinning gear produced a three-pound spotted weakfish. The next few casts also produced fish. I thought about my fly rod in Joel's boat and laid down my spinning rod in the midst of the action. Along with the heavy 9-weight rod and a Pflueger Model 1498 reel, I had a box of rudimentary red-and-white and green-and-white streamers on which I had taken bluefish. That Saturday morning and the next two mornings, I enjoyed some of the best speckled-trout fishing of my entire life. Almost every cast to the deep water next to the oyster bar produced a fish. By Monday literally every fly in my small collection had been mangled. Neither Joel nor I was really excited about being "rescued" on Monday afternoon and towed away from our sea trout paradise.

All good fishing trips are memorable, but what makes that one stand out is that I caught those fish on a fly. Since that time over twenty-five years ago, many other ordinary trips have been turned into lifelong memories because I had fly tackle with me. Although I don't mean to defame any other angling technique, because I still practice most of them, catching fish with a fly rod is just more fun.

Fly tackle requires you to get closer to the fish. You often see the strike, and you feel the fish because you're holding the line in your hand when the hook is set. In no other method of angling is line held between one's fingers while casting, retrieving, hooking, and fighting the fish. It is the fairest one-on-one contest in angling and the most personal way to catch fish. Fly fishing is, at the same time, both complex and primitive.

Whether you fish inshore or offshore, a fly rod in your tackle mix gives you a complete box of tools to work with. Just as a complete set of golf clubs enables you to hit a full repertoire of shots, fly tackle enhances your ability to play some aspects of the

Being stranded on an island by engine trouble can be a great experience . . . if you have a fly rod.

game of fishing—especially the finesse game. The appearance and movement of many baitfish and crustaceans can best be mimicked by flies.

I found out early on that to have fun with a fly rod you don't have to be able to cast ninety feet. Good distance-casting skills (see chapter 12) open up more opportunities, but new fly rodders who can get forty feet of line out of the boat and move the fly can catch fish.

In the 1970s and 1980s great schools of bluefish, often reaching twenty pounds, roamed the beaches and inlets north from the Outer Banks of North Carolina. On several occasions, while cruising beaches with friends in a four-wheel-drive, I saw the surf literally reddened with the blood of menhaden or sea trout. The big bluefish that caused the carnage were always easy marks for surf casters throwing bait or three-ounce metal squid. I caught my share of big blues on bait and metal, but it was the fly-caught fish that achieved immortality in my memory. One day at the south point at Cape Hatteras, blues had been crashing bait more than 150 feet off the beach—well out of casting range with a fly. After my friends and I had caught several large fish on spinning tackle, I couldn't stand it any longer. I waded wet—without waders—through the slough in chest-deep water until I stood on the outer bar in water no more than knee-deep. To my surprise, when I got there, I saw no fish. Over the noise of the surf I could hear faint calls of "Behind you. Come back . . . behind you. Come back."

When big bluefish showed up in droves on the North Carolina Outer Banks in the 1970s, anglers such as Joel Arrington discovered that fly fishing was the most enjoyable method of pursuing them.
Photograph by Tom Earnhardt

I turned around and looked at the beach, where my friends were pointing to the water at their feet. As I waded back toward them, large bluefish were cutting through bait all around me. When I got to the beach in shin-deep water, I was surrounded by bluefish. Any cast of more than thirty feet would have been too long. In the next hour I caught several "big shouldered" blues, weighing over fifteen pounds. Those fish would have been great sport on a spinning rod, but on a fly rod—a fun rod—they became lifelong memories.

Over the last quarter century, several hundred king mackerel have been brought into my boat. Almost all were caught on live baits. A few, however, have been caught on fly tackle, and those are the kings indelibly etched in my mind. A fly rod does add an extra dimension of enjoyment when catching any fish.

STRENGTH AND HANDICAPS OF NEW FLY RODDERS

New fly fishermen in salt water are coming from three groups. First, there are the freshwater fly fishermen with trout, panfish, or bass experience. Second, there is the angler with significant experience in salt water with other tackle, but no familiarity with fly-fishing gear. Finally, a surprisingly large number of new fly rodders come from a population of nonanglers who have never fly fished or been interested in salt-water fishing with other tackle. Each of these groups must deal with different advantages and handicaps.

Freshwater fly rodders sometimes have difficulty making the transition from their more delicate tackle to the stiffer, and more aggressive techniques used in the salt. Usually the biggest obstacle for such anglers is learning to make the change from confined ponds and streams to larger, more hostile expanses of water. Coastal winds for these fishermen are almost always a problem. One group of freshwater fly fishermen,

Spanish mackerel have become one of the favorite fly-rod quarry for many anglers who simply got tired of trolling for them . . . a great fun-rod fish.
Photograph by Tom Earnhardt

A surface feeding frenzy marks a great time to break out a fun rod.
Photograph by Tom Earnhardt

however, has less difficulty making the transition: the salmon and steelhead fishermen, who are used to the bigger rods and flies, and the heavier lines, used in salt water.

In my experience, the largest segment of new salty fly fishermen comes from the ranks of those with spin-fishing and conventional tackle experience. Teaching casting clinics over the years, I have heard the same refrain again and again: "I got tired of trolling for Spanish mackerel and dolphin. . . . There just had to be a better way."

The plus for anglers in this group is that they often know a lot about saltwater fish and their habits, and they are able to convert that knowledge to their benefit when they pick up a fly rod. The minus that afflicts many of these anglers is a litany of old habits. Because most have been used to applying lots of muscle when heaving heavy lures or bait, they have a hard time letting a fly rod do its work. For them the chief lesson that has to be learned is that in fly fishing there is far more finesse and much less muscle.

The final group of new entries, anglers with no fishing experience at all, are people looking for a new hobby, much in the way of those taking up golf, tennis, or photography for the first time. On the one hand, such anglers start with a clean slate and no bad habits. On the other hand, they have the burden of both learning fly-fishing technique and mastering the environment in which their new hobby will be practiced.

There are top dogs in every sport, but that fact of life has not kept millions from playing golf, tennis, or pickup basketball, or shooting sporting clays. Fly fishing in salt water is a sport that can be enjoyed by virtually anyone, especially women, children, and older anglers. It can be an addition to, and not a replacement of, other methods of taking fish. You can choose to gear up for only a few fish, such as stripers and redfish, or you can pursue a variety of opponents from brackish to blue water. Regardless of the group you belong to, fly fishing offers the greatest potential for enjoyment of any angling technique.

CHAPTER 3

LEARNING FROM "HEATHEN"

Many of the best saltwater fishermen I know have never held a fly rod in combat or have only a slight acquaintance with saltwater fly-fishing gear. It is ironic to me that some saltwater fly rodders, especially those new to the game, get so wrapped up in the sport that they actually begin to look down on nonfly fishermen: "Heathen" or "nonbelievers" are terms I have heard applied in only half jest. Although I firmly believe that saltwater fly-fishing skills will help to make anyone a better all-around angler, I have always looked for counsel and guidance to the great anglers who are less enamored with saltwater fly fishing than I.

Great fishermen come in two categories: the specialist and the generalist. Every town on the East, Gulf, and West Coast has local gurus who are simply the best. An example of a specialist in this category is Captain Norman Miller of Ocracoke, North Carolina, whose fish is the red drum (known locally as channel bass)—not just any red drum, but several hundred fish over forty pounds for his clients every season. His domain includes the beaches and shoals of Ocracoke Inlet and virtually all of the central Pamlico Sound. His peers also give him extraordinarily high marks for his innovative wreck-fishing techniques in nearshore waters.

Another great angler, but one you would have to classify as a generalist, is Claude Bain, director of the Virginia Saltwater Fishing Tournament. In the lower Chesapeake no one knows more about stripers, bluefish, cobia, spotted weakfish, tautog, and flounder. He is also very advanced in his knowledge of bluewater fish at the mouth of the Chesapeake, especially yellowfin tuna and white marlin. Bain is also the type of angler equally comfortable in the surf and in a modern center console.

Every region of the country has its own versions of Norman Miller and Claude Bain. All of these great anglers have several things in common. First, they understand their quarry—seasonal movement, temperature requirements, preferred foods, and the effect of tides. Their knowledge of winds and area shorelines always gives them options unavailable to most anglers. In all but the worst weather, they will know places where fish are to be found.

Such master anglers are adept at the use of bait and lures. They know how to hook and "swim" a bait for the most natural effect, whether it be shrimp, crabs, men-

Captain Norman Miller of Ocracoke knows as much about the habits of red drum as anyone on the North Carolina coast.
Photograph by Tom Earnhardt

haden, or finger mullet. Because they know the movement of natural baits, they are better at lure fishing. Depending on water temperature, they have a better sense of the speed at which an artificial should be retrieved. For example, when water temperature is in the 60s, spotted-weakfish experts may impart a darting action to plugs or plastic-tailed jigs. When the temperatures drop into the 50s, the same fishermen may "soak" a lure, meaning let it sink to the bottom, then move it ever so slightly. Not only do great anglers have a sixth sense about fish behavior, but most also keep very good records of their catches and the conditions under which they were made. In areas of the country where there are still relatively few experienced saltwater fly fishermen, there is much to be learned by questioning and observing the best "heathen."

Pete Allred, a Morehead City tackle-shop proprietor and fountain of information, helped me as much as anyone to "translate" conventional fishing knowledge in my region into fly-fishing success. On one occasion we were fishing for gray trout (common weakfish) in Pamlico Sound. We were catching fish in about twenty feet of water on slender, lead-bodied jigs manufactured under the name Stingsilvers. Pete happened to mention that the same lure was also his favorite for false albacore in the fall of the year, when they feed voraciously on silversides. It was only after Pete made the connection between small, slender lures and false albacore that I began to experiment with sparsely dressed bucktails that had bodies made of Mylar piping. My size-4 streamers, between an inch and a half and two inches in length, looked for all the world like Black-Nosed Dace streamers, which I had long used for trout in the mountains of western North Carolina. When the false albacore and bonito arrived in the fall of that same year, I had great success with flies because of the help of Pete Allred, a nonfly fisherman.

Saltwater fly fishermen should pay close attention to the lures used by successful anglers who use spinning and conventional tackle. This is a selection of productive lures and the flies that match them.
Photograph by Tom Earnhardt

Just by examining the favorite offerings of lure fishermen, fly rodders can often make better fly selections. Spanish mackerel and king mackerel have long been taken on lead-headed round lures that are the approximate diameter of a ballpoint pen. Such lures are produced under numerous trade names, including Gotcha and Sea Hawk. These lures, which have a dipping, feinting action, can be mimicked in action and size by the now-famous Clouser Sinking Minnow (see chapter 6 for more information on Clousers). The Clouser is also a terrific substitute for countless soft plastic-bodied jigs, which have been a mainstay for saltwater anglers seeking a variety of species. Weakfish, stripers, bluefish, flounder, and redfish can easily be taken by a properly presented Clouser using colors similar to those used in heavy lures— green/white, red/white, white/silver, pink/white, and so on.

Perhaps the most successful saltwater lure in history is the MirrOlure, which is a great imitation of small mullet and a variety of other inshore baitfish. Just knowing what colors and weights MirrOlure fishermen have selected, you can choose an equally good fly. A number of flies produce the same profile and motion in the water. Lefty's Deceiver, Fernandez's Sea-Ducer, and Popovic's Siliclone (see chapter 6 for more detail) are all good matches for the MirrOlure. It may not be as sexy as matching an aquatic insect hatch on a trout stream, but saltwater fly rodders who know how to match the "plastic hatch" will get results.

PURISTS, STAY HOME

Fly fishermen can be a cantankerous lot. Over the years I have had the good fortune to fish in a number of countries with some extraordinary anglers and characters. Several years ago a friend I had met in Europe planned a business trip to the United States around a few days of fishing with me in Montana. I had fished with him on his home turf and knew that he possessed great skill as a caster, fly tier, and stream reader. I also admired a trait that he and other European anglers often share—a tenacious dedication to the dry fly. For him fly fishing was not fly fishing unless it was with a dry fly.

On the Big Horn, Yellowstone, and several other rivers, his passion for fishing the dry fly proved frustrating to him and to those around him. We experienced times of high water and other conditions that were simply not conducive to the use of drys. While others and I were successful with nymphs and streamers, he refused to forsake his tiny floaters. Tenacity and principle are characteristics to be admired—to a point. My friend, and most like him, fully realize that their passion for doing it one way means self-imposed limits.

I have spent days on the bows of Keys skiffs in sub-hurricane-force winds in water that looked more like a vanilla milk shake than a gin-clear flat. On many of those days, when some frustrated captain suggested that it was time to give up the hunt for tarpon and head for the mangroves for snapper or to a bar for an adult beverage, I stood my ground. What my European friend and I have in common is a devotion to the sport of fly fishing on our own terms that sometimes keeps us from learning and, from a more practical standpoint, keeps us from catching more fish.

In saltwater fly fishing many tricks of the trade are practiced that freshwater fly anglers would never consider. A perfect example is chumming. Ground fresh fish or chunks of fish are released from a boat, or even from a jetty, on an outgoing tide. The trick is to keep the chum line, or slick, unbroken so that any fish entering or passing through the line will smell it and seek its source. (More about chumming later.) This is a technique accepted by most fly rodders for king mackerel, bluefish, sharks, and other species. Chumming is also practiced by some fly fishermen and guides in the tropics, who throw out pieces of fresh shrimp to attract bonefish.

No self-respecting fly fisherman in Maine, Pennsylvania, or Montana would chum for trout on a river with salmon eggs, worms, or crickets. Such long-recognized codes of conduct sometimes make it difficult for freshwater fly rodders to make the transition to salt water. Saltwater fly rodders understand that, for the most part, the ocean is a desert, and the use of fish-attracting techniques is necessary to bring fish within casting distance.

On many occasions I have experienced wonderful dolphin fishing using fly tackle. Dolphin are available in the Gulf of Mexico, around the Keys, and on the edge of the Gulf Stream far up the East Coast. With their iridescent blues, greens, and golds, they are among the most beautiful fish. Although I have caught dolphin off the coast of several states, my best fishing has been in my home waters near Cape Lookout, North Carolina. Often, after several days of a south or southeast wind, patches of sargassum will be blown within sight of land. I have caught a few dolphin moving from patch to patch blind casting, but most of my success has been as a result of the Judas-fish tactic. Using plastic squid or a ballyhoo strip, I troll near the sargassum mats until

The use of live baitfish, chum, and Judas fish is often necessary to bring fish into casting range. These amberjack are ready for anything thrown to them.
Photograph by Lefty Kreh

Judas fish and chum lines are often used to bring gamefish within casting range. They can be used separately or together.

a dolphin is hooked. The engines are killed, and the fish is played to within forty feet of the boat, where it is left as a Judas fish to attract its buddies. With or without a little chum, dolphin often stay well within casting distance for fly rodders. The same technique can be used for a variety of schooling fish, as well, including bluefish, Spanish mackerel, and cobia. Is the Judas-fish ploy a dirty trick, or smart angling?

In saltwater fly fishing there are many things considered unfair by anglers and by the IGFA (International Game Fish Association). In fly fishing no bait or scent is allowed on flies, and flies may not be trolled behind a boat if the fish is to be considered a "fly-caught" fish. To qualify for the record books, fish must be caught on leaders that include at least fifteen inches of "test tippet" and no more than twelve inches of wire or heavy-monofilament "shock tippet." (Leaders will be discussed in detail in chapter 9.) There are a number of other rules dealing with everything from gaffs to multiple hooks and flies.

I know the IGFA rules and generally adhere to them, but I also believe that fly fishing should be fun. On a number of occasions I have taken friends to wrecks where amberjack can be teased into fly-casting range. When fishing from large boats, I have sometimes used a two-and-a-half or three-foot shock tippet so that I could more easily control a large jack without gaffing it once it was brought to the boat. Had any fish been a world's record, it would never have been entered. A longer shock tippet makes sense to me in teaching situations, so that I can release fish in a manner safe for both fish and angler.

I hope my point has not been missed. Rules and standards are important, especially when it comes to maintaining the integrity of fishing records. Common sense must also be applied. If you aren't having fun, and aren't catching fish with some regularity, saltwater fly fishing can lose its luster fast.

My advice: Buy a good spin fisherman a cup of coffee and pick his brain. Grab your fly rod and head for the nearest chum line. Enjoy. . . .

PART II

WORKING WITH FORCES OF NATURE TO BECOME A BETTER ANGLER

CHAPTER 4

COASTAL BIOLOGY—
SPARTINA TO SARGASSUM

Having been a fisherman and an observer of coastal ecosystems for most of my life, I know of no word that is more evocative than "spartina." Spartina is the cordgrass rimming bays, sounds, and barrier islands on the East and Gulf coasts. Cordgrass is also found in some estuaries of the Pacific Coast states. Depending on the season, it is chartreuse, deep green, or amber. A spartina marsh is not just grass; it is also a filter, a sponge, a hiding place, a nesting place, and a food source. Spartina is, for a large number of coastal creatures, both the beginning and the staff of life.

Some fly fishing takes place in or near tidal marshes, but almost all quarry of fly rodders are affected by them. In some places footing in a salt marsh may be sure and firm. In other places the oil-black ooze of a marsh will suck your boots off. They are wild, wonderful places.

I promise that I will not force you to take Coastal Biology 101, but without a basic understanding of spartina and the inshore food web, your career as a saltwater fly rodder will be an undistinguished one. No trout fisherman is ever told to forget about those ridiculous little aquatic insects—mayflies, stoneflies, and caddisflies—or about the pH of water. On the contrary, a good trout fisherman is a biologist, and every good saltwater angler I know, whether bait fisherman or fly rodder, is to some degree an amateur marine scientist.

As a fly fisherman, you are, in the scheme of things, no more than an advanced predator. Your one advantage over other predators is that, being at the very top of the food chain, you have the option of targeting virtually all of the finfish as prey. Once you learn the rhythm of the tides and the seasonal movement of the fish, you have the option of catching shrimp eaters, crab eaters, and fish that feed on other finfish. Whether you devote most of your time to a single species or become a saltwater generalist, your success will be directly related to your knowledge of the ecosystems you frequent.

The great estuarine systems of the East and Gulf coasts are spawning and nursery areas for gamefish both large and small. Whether you study the Chesapeake Bay,

Spartina marshes from New England to Florida's Indian River and along the Gulf Coast are the beginning of the food web for most finfish and shellfish.
Photograph by Tom Earnhardt

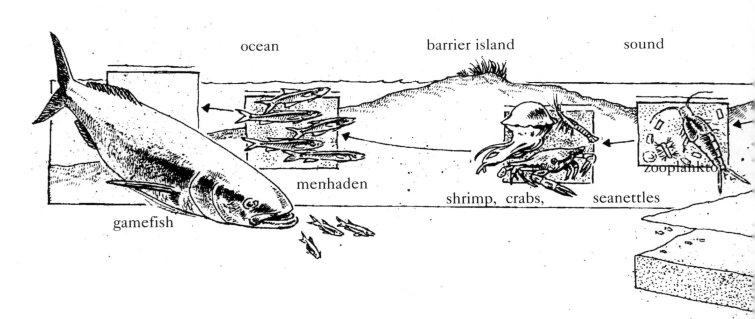

ocean   barrier island   sound

menhaden   shrimp, crabs,   zooplankton

gamefish   seanettles

Fly rodders must understand the food web from the tidal marsh to the open sea.

North Carolina's Pamlico Sound, Port Royal Sound in South Carolina, or a Louisiana marsh, you will draw many of the same conclusions. Roughly 90 percent of all coastal fish are directly related to or get their sustenance from the great estuaries rimmed by spartina. Common weakfish, speckled trout, redfish, and smaller fish such as croaker and spot are all directly tied to shallow estuaries. Along the East Coast and Gulf Coast, such gamefish as tarpon, cobia, Spanish mackeral, jack crevalle, and ladyfish all come into the estuaries to spawn or feed. In the fall, as estuaries begin to cool down, immature gamefish and a variety of baitfish begin pouring out of inlets, only to be met by larger gamefish looking for a feast: King mackerel, false albacore, bonito, amberjack, and dolphin are among the waiting predators.

The shallow estuaries are in many ways a nutrient soup. Organic and inorganic matter moves down coastal rivers into estuaries. This matter, along with decaying spartina and sunlight, allows for the formation and growth of countless tiny organisms known as plankton. Plankton is divided into two categories: First, there is zooplankton, which is that part of the plankton that consists of tiny animals; and second, there is phytoplankton, which is that part of the plankton that consists of plants or plant-like organisms, such as algae. This plankton, born out of the marriage of sun and the rich nutrient soup, is the beginning of the food chain for many of the crustaceans, including shrimp and crabs. Plankton also provides food for most of the mollusks, such as oysters, clams, snails, and even squids (mollusks that have no shells).

Many of the most significant food fishes or gamefish, such as menhaden (also known as bunker and fatback), mullet, and mud minnows (also known as mummi-

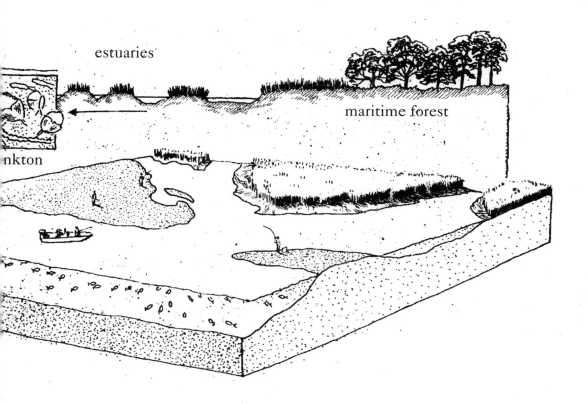

chogs), and the large category of slender minnows known as "glass minnows" are, for the most part, plankton feeders. Some, such as mullet and menhaden, are primarily phytoplankton feeders. Finally, another major source of food for larger gamefish is juvenile gamefish. The smallest bluefish, red drum, and sea trout—also in the same food web, but just further up—are themselves then eaten by their larger cousins.

Even though many fish sought by fly rodders are predators that will eat a number of things around them, such as crabs, menhaden, or shrimp, saltwater fish, like trout in fresh water, will sometimes key in on a favored food. This is especially true on a seasonal basis. Cobia and large red drum may feed voraciously on menhaden before entering shallow estuaries in the spring and early summer. Their primary food sources may then switch to various species of swimming crabs. On the North Carolina coast, many of my live-baiting friends do extremely well during the spring and summer using live shrimp on spotted weakfish, but prefer three-inch finger mullet for weakfish in the fall. Even the time of the month may dictate what certain fish are eating. For example, in the waters behind the South Carolina and Georgia barrier islands, red drum can reach areas frequented by burrowing fiddler crabs only during the heavier tides that occur during the new moon and full moon. The addition of an extra foot of water allows redfish to move into these areas not usually available to them. Fly rodders have found that in shallow areas during heavier tides, redfish crave a crab pattern.

Whether you fish Barnegat Bay in New Jersey, behind Hilton Head in South Carolina, or in Galveston Bay, you must learn the rhythm of the estuary. All of these areas have essentially the same types of food available for gamefish—various crustaceans and small finfish. As an angler, you must learn what your favorite quarry is

Tidal creeks usually provide the fly rodder a number of options as the seasons change. Photograph by Tom Earnhardt

Mats of sargassum nearshore and offshore provide cover and food for a wide variety of gamefish.
Photograph by Lefty Kreh

keying in on during a particular season. You must also be aware that many of these foods change in size during the season. Mullet, menhaden, crabs, herring, small mackerel, and other baitfish all vary in size during the season. Fly rodders should be prepared to change fly sizes accordingly. Years ago I noticed that the silversides imitations that I used for false albacore and Spanish mackerel in the fall—usually two and a half inches in length—were often far too large to imitate the silversides of spring. As you will see in the section on flies, I do not believe that an exact imitation is necessary; however, I do try to match the approximate sizes and shapes of the baitfish or crustaceans I am trying to imitate.

NEARSHORE AND OFFSHORE "GRASS BEDS"

Just as spartina serves as a place of shelter and a source of nutrients for countless inshore fish, mollusks, and crustaceans, the same can be said for sargassum, the wonderful green-gold weed widely distributed in warmer waters around the globe.

Sargassum mats are the home to juvenile fish and crustaceans and can hold gamefish nearshore and offshore.

Whether off Florida, the Carolinas, or the mouth of the Chesapeake, large patches of sargassum can be pushed relatively close to shore by winds. In the Gulf Stream itself or over the shallower waters of the continental shelf, sargassum is also a sanctuary for countless tiny creatures, including shrimp, crabs, eels, tiny file fish, and many other tasty morsels for larger creatures. Because sargassum, an algae, is the home of so many delectable foods for larger fish, mats of the weed can attract a wide variety of gamefish preferred by fly rodders. The most obvious, of course, is the dolphin. On calm days in midsummer I look for rows, patches, and mats of sargassum in my search for dolphin. The usual fish that I find are the two- to five-pound "shingle" dolphin. The real prizes, however, are the pairs, a bull and a cow, which will often weigh over twenty-five pounds. Larger dolphin can eat smaller dolphin and flying fish that are often in the same areas. Under sargassum mats I have also found amberjack, cobia,

Although not spectacular jumpers like dolphin, tripletail, like the one above, and a variety of other fish are attracted to sargassum mats and other floating debris.
Photograph by Tom Earnhardt

and a most unappreciated fly-rod fish, tripletail. Very quickly, the savvy angler understands that the food web built around sargassum expands to include yellowfin tuna, wahoo, sailfish, white marlin, and blue marlin. In later chapters there will be more discussion of some of the techniques and tricks available to nearshore and offshore anglers seeking dolphin, sailfish, and other great gamefish.

STRUCTURE FISHING

It would be unfair to leave a discussion of inshore and offshore habitat without a look at the importance of large, fixed structures. Many new anglers are unaware that much of the ocean is a desert, and most fish are found on or near "oases" in the desert. Sargassum, or even floating debris, is for all practical purposes floating structure. Fixed structures such as sunken ships, light towers, oil rigs, irregular rocky bottom, or coral reefs will all hold gamefish. Sport fishermen who have Loran C or one of the

Artificial reefs and sunken ships are complete ecosystems that are home to the smallest and the largest sea creatures.

several ground-position locating systems on their boats use them not only for navigation but also for finding structures. No skipper worth his salt ventures offshore without a list of coordinates or compass headings that will help him or her locate artificial reefs and other significant structures. Charts listing such locations in your area are often available from state agencies dealing with marine resources or from fishing clubs. Such structures can be the fly rodder's best friend, since in season they hold a wide variety of fantastic fly-rod targets, including amberjack, king mackerel, dolphin, African pompano, barracuda, and other structure-loving critters. Each wreck, reef, light tower, or drilling platform is almost a closed ecosystem in that each has shelter and food for the smallest to the largest creatures in the food web.

The next time you drive over a high bridge in a coastal area that allows you to see a vast expanse of spartina, or the next time you are walking on a beach and find bits of sargassum in the surf, remember that these are not just ordinary plants. For a number of years I have seen the same bumper sticker in a number of states that says it all in a few words: "No wetlands, no seafood." Because of the direct relationship between salt marshes and roughly 90 percent of all saltwater gamefish, one could expand the bumper sticker a bit: "No wetlands, no seafood, no fly fishing." Personally, I could give up fried flounder before I could give up fly fishing.

CHAPTER 5

TIDES AND WIND

I have a friend who is a real ancient mariner. Captain Donald Willis was born eighty years ago in the Outer Banks community where my wife and I have a vacation home. In those years he has been a "coasty" (coast guardsman), an employee of the Army Corps of Engineers, and the skipper of a research vessel for a major university. He walks through our yard almost every day on the way to his wooden skiff. Rarely a day passes that he doesn't spend time sitting in that small boat or clamming in the marsh across the channel. Nothing on the water goes by him unnoticed.

Captain Donald Willis, shown here with the author's son Izaak, listens to the "whether service" and then makes a forecast based on his observations and instincts.
Photograph by Tom Earnnardt

Donald is my official weatherman. He listens to the "whether service" ("whether it's going to blow, or whether it's not") and then makes a forecast based on his own observations and instincts. He has learned from experience that on the water there are no guarantees, not even when they are based on satellites and computers. He once told me that most upstate fishermen (outsiders) with their fancy boats are like Ulysses' crew when it came to understanding the wind.

According to Donald's version of the Greek myth, "Ulysses had four bags of wind. The bag he opened most often contained the west wind, the kindest of winds. Because the other three bags contained problem winds, he ordered his crew never to open them except on his instruction. The north wind was cold and treacherous. The east wind often blew ill. The south wind, although warm, was unpredictable."

"One night," said Captain Donald, "while Ulysses slept, his crew opened all three bags out of curiosity, and a great storm arose, tossing his ship onto the rocks. Ulysses was furious that his orders had been disobeyed."

"What's that got to do with fishermen and boaters from upstate?" I asked.

"Most weekend fishermen with all their electronic gear know very little about the wind—how it affects currents, tides, and fish. If you gave most of them Ulysses' four bags to work with, they would be completely lost—because there is no owner's manual," mused Donald.

After listening to my local TV weather person give the weekend coastal forecast on Thursday evening, I often call Donald to get the "official" forecast. He knows that air and water temperatures have to be considered. He also knows that when predicting sea conditions inshore, one cannot possibly separate wind and tides.

Donald is a realist and knows there will always be wind in the region. The question is, how much? There is on the Banks an old saying that reflects the belief that wind is a constant: "When the wind stops blowing on the Outer Banks, everybody falls down."

If you want to fly fish in salt water, you must understand the tides and learn to deal with wind. There are certain days when fly fishing is not possible, and I have experienced those days in the Bahamas, in the Chesapeake Bay, and virtually every other place I have spent any length of time. High winds make casting difficult, and they can also turn shallow waters into soup. The more you learn about fish in various locales, however, the more you will understand that in all but the worst weather you will be able to find lee shores or protected bays and inlets that are fishable.

TIDES

A quick review of how tides work might be helpful. Tides are often referred to as lunar tides, but this term is misleading. Tides are caused by the gravitational pull of both the moon and, to a lesser degree, the sun. The biggest tides—and from the angler's viewpoint often the best tides—occur a few days before, during, and after a full moon and new moon. These are called spring tides, and there are two sets of them each month. The moon travels around the Earth in roughly twenty-eight days. During the time when the moon and sun are most directly in line with the earth— around the time of the new moon and full moon—tides will be highest because the gravitational pull of the sun and the moon exercise their effects in concert.

Neap Tide

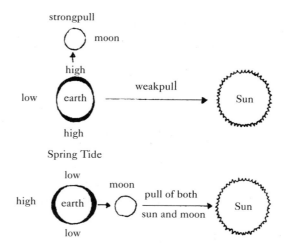

When the sun and moon are in line during the new moon or full moon, spring tides occur. When the sun and moon are at right angles, weaker tides (neap tides) are the result.

During the first quarter and the last quarter of the moon, the moon and the sun will be at right angles to each other so that their gravitational forces are actually working against each other, causing smaller tides, known as neap tides. Although fish can be caught at any time of the month, many anglers like to plan trips around the bigger tides, because when greater quantities of water move through flats, marshes, and inlets, there is more movement and channeling of baitfish, crustaceans, and other food. Spring tides also reach far back into areas not affected by neap tides, thereby making it possible to fish in areas not available around the first and last quarter of the moon.

With a little knowledge of the tides, you can make your own predictions about water flow and the accessibility of certain fishing areas. For example, in most locations there is a complete tidal change—two highs and two lows—during a span of approximately twenty-five hours. Under normal conditions tides will therefore be one hour later each day than they were the day before. Thus, if high tide is at noon on Saturday, the high on Sunday will be around one P.M. Also, because the strongest part of the tide—both incoming (flood tide) and outgoing (ebb tide)—is directly between the high and the low, most anglers like to fish an hour and a half on either side of the peak flow that occurs between the two highs and the two lows each day. These periods of major flow are the times during which many saltwater fish will be most likely to feed. This is true whether you are fishing in an area where there is very little tidal change, such as the Texas coast—where tidal changes can be around a foot and a half—or whether you are fishing on the North Carolina Outer Banks, where tidal change may average between three and four feet. The simple fact is that tides trigger feeding activity.

Even if you are fishing ten miles offshore over a wreck, or ten miles up the coastal river, tides can still have a profound effect on feeding activity. Researchers have told me that miles offshore, in water over wrecks sixty feet deep, the addition of three more feet of water during high tide will not only increase "head pressure" (deeper water means more pressure) but can also cause currents around a wreck to change direction. The lateral lines and other sensory organs of most fish are extremely sensitive and detect these changes. Slight current changes can also cause smaller bait and crustaceans to move or change position, making them more vulnerable to larger predators.

Another fact about tides you may want to remember is that every two weeks tides repeat themselves. Thus, if you return to the same area in fourteen days, the phase of the tide should be similar. If you experienced a high tide around say, 10 A.M., fourteen days later high tide will occur close to the same time.

Anglers who have spent any time on the coast know that tides vary even between nearby locations. For this reason tide tables are available at marinas, motels, and restaurants wherever fishermen eat and congregate. Tide tables usually give corrections for different locations in the area. For example, assume that high tide at "Rock Point" will be at two o'clock in the afternoon. Five miles to the east at "Sunny Point," high tide will be at one o'clock. Five miles to the west of "Rock Point," at "Hidden Bay," high tide will occur at three. No matter what coastline you are fishing, such variations will occur along relatively small areas, and tide tables can help you to move to an area where the action is likely to be better. This is why you will often hear a guide say, "Things seem to have slowed down here, but if we make a fifteen-minute run down to Hidden Bay, we can catch the last of the good tides."

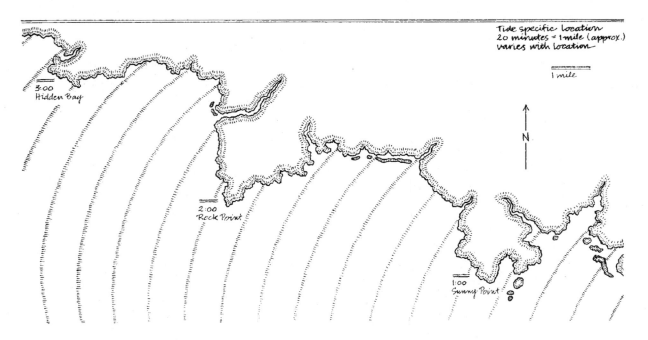

Tidal action can vary significantly even over a small area. Be aware of time variation of tides in your area.

WIND TIDES

I titled this chapter "Tides and Wind" because you simply can't separate them. Winds can also cause tides or have a profound effect on lunar/solar tides. If a steady wind is blowing in the same direction as the movement of tide, water levels can be several inches or several feet higher than the expected normal high. I can remember many days in which the wind was blowing in the opposite direction of the tidal flow, causing the tide to be less than expected or even causing it to disappear altogether. Anglers should consider such "wind tides" as significant as the gravitational tides because of the effect they have on fishing. For example, along the Texas coast a wind out of the northern quadrant will blow water away from the coast, causing more flats areas to be exposed and often producing better fishing for redfish and sea trout. Steady winds out of the southern quadrant on the same section of Texas coast can push an extra couple feet of water into the area, making fish more difficult to spot and migration patterns more difficult to predict.

The wind tide I most remember occurred when I was in high school, on a large-mouth bass fishing trip to Currituck Sound with my father. The first day of the trip was ideal—moderate winds and great fishing. That night the wind began to blow hard out of the north. When we arrived at the dock the next morning, our guide's boat, and in fact all boats at the dock, were stuck hard in the mud, and the nearest water was probably one hundred feet from the end of the dock. The wind had literally blown all water out of the sound.

The more time you spend observing the effects of wind and tide, the better you will be able to predict the movements of fish and bait, especially in areas where you fish the most. You will learn which flats, holes, sloughs, or inlets are most productive during tidal changes. You will learn which fish move into areas during higher water and what they are likely to feed on. You will learn where fish congregate in deeper water, waiting for food to be swept to them during a falling tide.

You will also learn exceptions to the "rules." For example, I like to look for cobia at slack tide around buoys, not during the peak flow times. At both high and low slack tide, before the change of tide, cobia, during the spring and fall of the year, like to swim in a counterclockwise motion around buoys. A well-presented Deceiver or a large crab imitation will most likely draw a strike from a buoy-circling cobia. This is just one of many exceptions to the general rule that fishing is best during peak flows.

Like most busy people who take their fishing time when they can get it, I often find myself fishing when tides or wind direction are less than optimal. Other factors, such as barometric pressure and the passing of a storm front, can also affect fishing success. Plan the best you can with the winds and tides available to you, and then believe that your fishing trip is going to be successful. Most fish feed every day! The best fishing often comes when we least expect it.

CHAPTER 6

THE FOOD CHAIN
AND IMITATIONS
Flies Do It Better

Not too long ago there were relatively few flies for saltwater fly fishing when compared with the thousands available for freshwater species, especially trout. How things have changed! Catalogs now have as many pages of saltwater flies as those available for fresh water. For many anglers fly tying or the acquisition of beautiful flies becomes almost as satisfying as fishing itself. Unfortunately, great flies will not automatically make you a better angler.

Most of the flies I use I tie myself, except for those I spirit from the boxes of friends. On any given trip I carry an arsenal of feathered options for a wide range of species. Several years back I was fishing with Captain Dennis Hammond within sight of the gantries at the Kennedy Space Center. Dennis and I were fishing for tripletail and jack near the point of Cape Canaveral. As so often happens in saltwater fishing, we were surprised to find ourselves suddenly surrounded by schools of the "wrong" fish, false albacore. Since Alberts are one of my favorite Mid-Atlantic fish, I had the situation covered with a variety of Clousers and epoxy Surf Candies. I don't know of any two better types of flies for false albacore. True to form, the albacore ate my offerings.

Captain Hammond smiled and suggested that the precise imitations of glass minnows I was using were simply not necessary for his albacore. He handed me the simplest saltwater fly I have ever used. Hammond's albacore fly was nothing more than a stainless size-4 hook dressed with a dozen white bucktail hairs tied to the shank with red nylon thread. The entire fly was an inch and a half in length and had no eyes, and nothing to add flash. In the next half hour I caught three albacore on Hammond's ultrasimple white bucktail.

Even though I believe in simplicity, unlike Captain Hammond, I don't always practice what I preach. With a few notable exceptions, most fish in salt water can be caught on relatively simple patterns if those patterns are the right size, put in front of the fish, and moved properly. Less than beautiful flies work just fine. When I think

Anglers should always pay close attention to the size of bait being pursued by gamefish. Here false albacore can be seen chasing silversides. Photograph by Tom Earnhardt

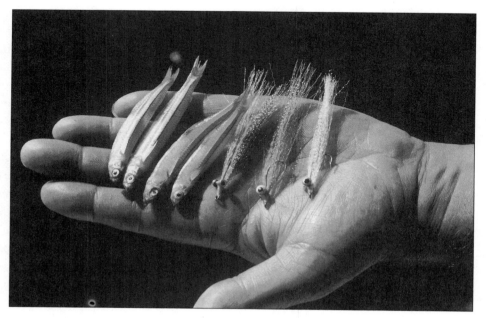

These Clouser Minnows are an excellent match, both in size and shape, for the silversides.
Photograph by Tom Earnhardt

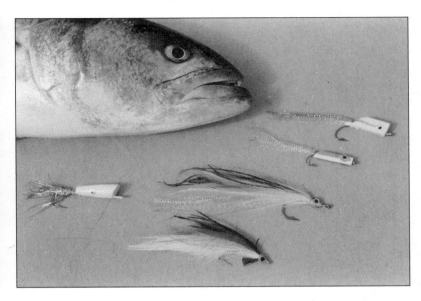

Bluefish like simple patterns. Photograph by Tom Earnhardt

back over the past thirty years of fly fishing the salt, I can remember tarpon, stripers, bluefish, weakfish, redfish, and many other critters that ate my early, unpretentious creations. Great flies may give an angler confidence, but great presentation is far more significant.

When I talk about simple flies, I am not talking about flies that lack innovation. The Deceiver, in all its variations, is a simple fly. Dan Blanton's Whistlers are uncomplicated flies with bead eyes that "push" water. The use of painted or "stick-on" eyes is a common sense addition to most flies. Eyes are thought to provoke strikes. Many flies used in the Northeast are tied with ostrich or marabou, causing the flies to breathe and pulsate in rough water. The use of epoxy in many flies was a brilliant but simple step. Almost all saltwater patterns are now tied with synthetic materials that add flash. For example, virtually all my Clouser Minnows are tied with synthetics, such as Ultra Hair, to reflect more light. Simplicity does not mean that flies should be tied with less than the best available materials.

A cast net is a good way to collect baitfish so that flies can be matched in both size and shape.
Photograph by Tom Earnhardt

A look at the real thing is always helpful. Here a finger mullet is examined from the front and from the side. Photograph by Tom Earnhardt

Perhaps the major exception to my "simple fly" rule is the evolution of realistic crab patterns. Prior to the modern crab patterns, some fish such as permit and mutton snapper were deemed almost uncatchable on traditional patterns. Although they are still difficult quarry for any fly rodder, the advent of super-realistic crab patterns such as Del Brown's Merkin and George Anderson's McCrab have made permit catchable. The same realistic crab patterns have also helped open up new redfish territories where the fish are keyed in on fiddlers or small blue crabs.

CHOOSING FLIES THAT WORK

Whether you buy or tie flies, there are certain things that all good saltwater flies have in common. In this chapter I have listed and photographed my Top Ten saltwater flies. I sincerely believe that armed with these ten patterns, or similar ones, in a variety of colors and sizes, I can catch the vast majority of fish available to saltwater fly rodders. These flies represent the "basic food groups" eaten by most gamefish. Any good collection must include a pattern that represents menhaden, herring, and shad. These fish, which are essentially the same shape, are found worldwide. No saltwater fisherman should be found without a good mullet fly. Finger mullet are a staple for redfish, sea trout, stripers, and a variety of other fish on all North American coasts. Any Top Ten list has flies mimicking slender, schooling baitfish, which anglers have grouped together as "silversides," "glass minnows," or "rain minnows." Some good crustacean imitations of shrimp and crabs are also a must. Any list should also have patterns that can imitate small eels or squid.

The most important flies listed in my Top Ten are Lefty's Deceiver and the Clouser Minnow. Both of these patterns are methods of tying as opposed to imitations

Earnhardt's Top Ten flies for the East and Gulf coasts (from left to right, beginning at the top). All of the following flies should be carried in a variety of sizes and colors: Clouser Minnow, Surf Candy, Whistler, Lefty's Deceiver, Crazy Charlie, Deerhair Slider, Skipping Bug, Del Brown's Merkin, Sea-Ducer, and Bend Back.
Photograph by Tom Earnhardt

of a specific fish. The Deceiver can be tied in very small or very large sizes and can be bulky or sparse. Depending on the way they are tied, Deceivers can represent silversides, menhaden, mullet, or pinfish. Deceivers have caught everything from weakfish to marlin. When Lefty Kreh developed this fly for stripers in the late fifties around Crisfield, Maryland, he was looking for a fly that was foul-proof. You will notice that the large collar that extends back beyond the bend of the hook keeps feathers and longer materials of the fly from swinging back and fouling on the hook.

Bob Clouser's Deep Minnow was developed by Susquehanna smallmouth guide Bob Clouser. This very simple pattern with dumbbell lead eyes can also be tied in a variety of shapes and sizes. Clousers in combinations of light green and white make terrific imitations of silversides and are my favorite flies for false albacore, bonito, and Spanish mackerel. Larger Clousers are good for everything from stripers to king mackerel. Because the "barbell" eyes cause the hook to ride up, the Clouser can also be hopped across shallow flats and given the action of a shrimp. One of my favorite flies for redfish is a root-beer-colored (red-brown) Clouser, which makes a great shrimp imitation. Like the Deceiver pattern already mentioned, the Clouser Minnow is also relatively foul-proof since the wing of the fly rides above the hook. If the fish of the world have a chance to vote on purgatory for anglers, I am convinced that Lefty Kreh and Bob Clouser already have reserved rooms. The Deceiver and

Clouser Minnow, in various forms and shapes, have accounted for more fish in salt water than any other patterns of which I am aware.

There is no question that flies are better than ever because of the availability of modern tying materials. A couple of decades ago saltwater flies were tied with combinations of bucktail and saddle hackles. Later, tiers began to mix deer hair, ostrich and peacock herl, and other natural materials. Now few flies are constructed without some high-tech materials, such as Ultra Hair, Flashabou, Krystal Flash, and other fish-mimicking materials. Epoxy and clear silicone have found their way into many of the better flies available today. The undisputed master of silicone and epoxy is tier Bob Popovics, the New Jersey restaurateur who has created such flies as Surf Candies, Siliclones, Rubber Candies, and Ultra Shrimp. Bob is another great tier who will most assuredly gain a place in fish purgatory.

If you are new to saltwater fly fishing and are building a fly collection, keep in mind the target species that you will spend most of your time pursuing. Identify their main prey and then get a relatively simple collection of flies in several sizes and colors. My fly boxes are now full of flies, many of them quite beautiful, that will probably never enter salt water because I also carry a number of simple, proven patterns that I stick with.

No matter what flies you use, make sure you protect them. I keep most of my flies, whether bought or tied, in boxes with hooks secured in plastic foam linings. Saltwater flies placed loosely in fly boxes tend to wad up, mat, and lose their shape. If you don't use foam-lined boxes to protect your flies, then they should be stored in plastic sleeves available at many fly shops.

HOOKS AND BARBS

Over the last twenty years I have heard the debate over whether saltwater flies should be tied on stainless-steel, cadmium-coated, enamelled, or bronzed hooks. Some anglers believe that stainless hooks, if broken off and left in a fish, will stay there forever. They believe that bronzed hooks or enameled hooks with a base of conventional (carbon) steel will rust out in a relatively short period of time, leaving the fish hook free. Although I'm sure this argument will continue in the years to come, I, for one, am a proponent of stainless steel hooks for most flies, and there are several reasons for my position. A bronzed hook or any other coated hook will rust if it has been placed in salt water. A rusting hook will discolor the fly and often other flies around it in your fly box. Stainless steel, on the other hand, can be used and then placed in your fly box to be used again.

In the interest of fish and angling safety, most anglers I know bend down the barbs on all hooks. Many of the newer models of saltwater hooks that I buy actually have tiny barbs or no barbs at all. I'm convinced that barbless hooks, or hooks with the barbs mashed down, will in most situations work free quickly if they have been broken off in a fish. Therefore, why not use stainless hooks?

I have also found, and believe, that barbless or semibarbless hooks penetrate the mouths of most fish easily, whether it be a tarpon or a bluefish. Barbless and semi-barbless hooks do not fall out while the fish is being played, but it is much easier to release a fish from a barbless or semibarbless hook at the side of your boat. Equally

Barbs on hooks should always be bent down with a pair of pliers. New hooks should always be sharpened and then checked frequently during use. Always push the file toward the point. Photograph by Tom Earnhardt

important, it is much easier to release an angler hooked with a barbless hook. I have been stuck in the arms, neck, head, and butt on various occasions over the years, either by my own ineptitude or by the miscue of a fellow angler. I can testify from experience that the barbless hooks feel better being removed. Aah!

SHARPENING HOOKS

All good saltwater fly fishermen can agree on one thing: Sharpen all hooks! Whether you fish for tarpon with concrete jaws or rubbery-lipped redfish, a sharp hook will improve your chances. I have acquired a habit of carrying a small hook file in my pocket, whether I am fly fishing or using conventional tackle. A few strokes on top of the hook and on both sides *moving toward the point* will almost always improve hook sharpness and penetration. Some anglers are fastidious about always "triangulating" the point or making a diamond-shaped cutting point. Hooks with cutting points will more easily penetrate the fish's mouth. From personal experience I find that the only time I go out of my way to put cutting edges on a hook is when I am using larger sizes (2/0 to 6/0) or when I am using smaller hooks made with heavy-diameter wire. I believe that smaller-diameter hooks (sizes 1/0 and smaller) will penetrate well when they are simply *debarred* and *sharpened*. When sharpening hooks, you should take care not to make the point long and slender, since such points tend to break or roll when they hit a bony spot in a fish's mouth.

Most of the major hook manufacturers, including Mustad, Tiemco, Partridge, Eagle Claw, and others, now offer chemically sharpened hooks for saltwater use. These hooks are for most species "good to go" out of the box. From habit and experience, however, I still like to give every hook I use a few swipes with a good hook file. While I am fishing, I also try to remember to check the point to make sure that it has not been rolled, broken, or bent during casting or while being retrieved across a shell-studded bottom.

FLIES AS ART

Although I firmly believe that a few fly patterns fished well are all that most fly fishermen need, some magnificent compilations of the fly tier's art are available for those who want more precise and exact imitations. Even though such fish as bluefish and jack crevalle will eat almost any big fly that is presented well, some anglers believe that as a matter of "courtesy" they should use handsome flies. Lefty Kreh's *Saltwater Fly Patterns* and Dick Stewart and Farrow Allen's *Flies for Saltwater* are perhaps the best books available for anglers who want to see the latest and best in saltwater fly patterns. During the preparation of this book I went through my library on fly fishing carefully. One book that I had almost forgotten was *Salt Water Flies*, by Kenneth Bay, published in 1972. Although the pictures were printed in black and white and contain no Clouser Minnows or realistic crab patterns, the book includes many patterns that are popular today, and others that are clearly precursors of more innovative present-day patterns. What stands out, however, is that Mr. Bay's book and the best of modern pattern books all contain flies that replicate the important baitfish, crustaceans, and other prey. Fly fishermen must know the "food groups" and be prepared to match them.

Even after you have boxes of superb flies, remember that, more than anything else, your success depends upon presentation, which is a combination of placement and movement (more about presentation in chapter 13). The next time you change fly patterns several times and fish still fail to take your offering, you might think of Captain Dennis Hammond and his simple, all-bucktail glass-minnow imitation. Most of the fish we seek in the brine are top-of-the-food-chain, aggressive predators that will eat when given the opportunity. Keep it simple.

PART III

TACKLE AND ACCESSORIES
Keeping It Simple

CHAPTER 7

FLY RODS
A Very Subjective Decision

Having followed the development of saltwater fly rods through several "generations," I am now convinced that the same people who name cars for Detroit also moonlight as namers of fly rods. Why else would you have names of rods and series of rods such as Presidential, RPL-X, PM-10, Horizon, IMX, GLX, Imperial, XD Series, and Formula XL? Today's manufacturers, using state-of-the-art materials and equipment, have without question developed the finest array of casting tools ever available to saltwater fly fishermen—or to any fly fishermen, for that matter. Among those marketing or building fly rods for saltwater use are Sage, Orvis, G. Loomis, Thomas & Thomas, Lamiglas, Penn, R. L. Winston, Scott, Powell, Redington, St. Croix, Fenwick, L. L. Bean, and Cabela's.

Buying your first saltwater rod can be confusing enough, given all the choices and options, but it gets even more confusing when you hear the "experts" describe the capabilities of new rods. From time to time various fly-fishing magazines have experts cast and then describe comparable fly rods from different manufacturers. When I read the ratings given to rods, I always think of wine tasters trying to describe good wines. Experts often gush about fly rods with phrases such as "light and supple," "heavy in the butt," "needs more heft," "powerful and deft," "surprisingly light touch," and finally, "feels like a noodle but has surprising capabilities."

When you buy any fly rod, you are merely buying a flexible lever that propels your fly line, which in turn pulls your fly through the air. Manufacturers rate fly rods for use with 1- to 15-weight fly lines in accordance with standards set out by the AFTMA (American Fishing Tackle Manufacturers Association). The smaller the number, the lighter the line it will propel through the air. In order to determine what rating or number should be assigned to a rod, manufacturers determine what size line it will propel comfortably through the air. Lines are given their ratings by weighing the first thirty feet, exclusive of the level tip. Thus, for each fly rod there is a corresponding fly line that should be used for proper balance. Rods rated 1 and 2 have light actions for light lines and small flies. Rods with the classifications 3 through 6

Fish such as the false albacore held by the author can be hooked and landed on a 6- or 7-weight rod, but an 8- to 10- weight rod is preferable because the fish will have a much greater chance of survival. Choose enough rod for the fish you are seeking.
Photograph by Lefty Kreh

would encompass most of the most popular trout rods and panfish rods. Rods with line classifications of 7 are still freshwater rods but do have limited saltwater application. Number-8 rods are generally considered the beginning of rods suitable for salt water. Eight-weight rods will handle moderate winds and medium-size flies. Rods rated for 9- and 10-weight lines are the workhorses of the coastal fly-fishing community since they are used for a variety of fish, including permit, bluefish, king mackerel, albacore, bonito, stripers, and countless other medium-size fish. Rods in the 11 and 12 categories are powerful tools that can still be excellent for casting. Such rods are used for large tarpon, amberjack, cobia, and even sailfish. They may also be need-ed for fish requiring big flies in heavy surf or deep water. Rods rated 13 through 15 will cast a fly line, but they are best known as heavyweight fish-fighting tools for large sailfish, marlin, and tuna. These "heavyweights" are generally shorter than most other saltwater rods.

CHARACTERISTICS OF SALTWATER FLY RODS

If you already have a number-8 or -9 rod that you use for largemouth bass or salmon fishing, then you may already have the rod you need for saltwater fishing. You must keep in mind, however, that there are some very clear distinctions between rods designed for fresh water and rods used in the salt. I have been asked many times at casting clinics if Granddad's old bamboo rod can be used for stripers. The answer is almost invariably no for several reasons. First, I do not consider a rod fit for salt water unless it has oversize guides—stripping guides, snake guides, and a large tip. Even in rods rated 7 to 9 the first large guide, or stripping guide, should be at least twelve mm in diameter. Many of my number-9 and -10 rods have two stripping guides, one being a sixteen-mm guide and the next being a twelve-mm guide. All snake guides used on saltwater rods should be made of corrosion-resistant material and be size 5 or 6 the entire length of the rod. Tips should have an opening at least equal to the size of the smallest snake guide. Most older bass and salmon rods, and many new ones, have guides that are far too small and fragile for saltwater use. Larger guides are necessary because saltwater fish, generally being stronger and faster than those found in fresh

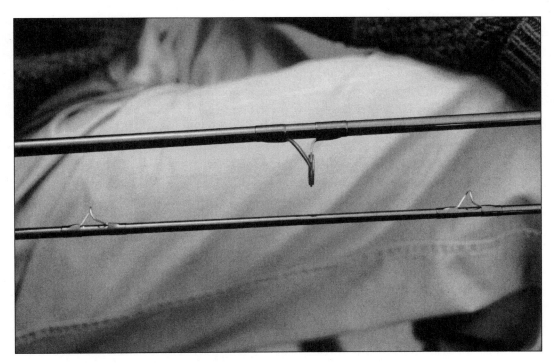

No rod can be considered a saltwater fly rod, regardless of its line-weight designation, if it does not have large strip-ping guides and large snake guides. Photograph by Tom Earnhardt

Saltwater fly rods normally have larger cork grips in the half-wells or full-wells shape. Note that the reel seats are of the up-locking variety and that the extension butts are relatively short. Long extensions only get in the way.
Photograph by Tom Earnhardt

water, often take line so fast that knots are formed as the fly line leaves the deck of your boat or shooting basket. A small knot can go through guides of a modern saltwater fly rod but would never go through the small guides found on most freshwater equipment. Another reason for the larger guides is that they allow for better casting, since the larger openings generally mean less friction on a moving fly line.

All hardware on modern saltwater rods should resist the effects of saltwater corrosion. It is especially important that the reel seat is not only corrosion resistant but heavy enough to accommodate larger saltwater reels and the pressure put on those reels by larger, stronger fish. Although there is plenty of debate about what size and shape the cork handle should be, most anglers prefer a longer and sometimes larger-diameter handle on saltwater rods than those found on most freshwater rods. Most manufacturers of rods choose a "half-wells" or "full-wells" shaped cork handle. Rods for salt water use usually have a two-inch permanent extension butt of cork or rubber. They do not get in the way while casting and can provide extra comfort when playing a strong fish. Larger, four- to eight-inch extension butts can get in the way and are rarely used.

CHOOSING A ROD

In the fifties and sixties saltwater fly rods were generally made of fiberglass. Some anglers, like the great Joe Brooks, did use well-made bamboo rods in the salt with success. Both glass and bamboo are, by today's standards, very heavy and slow. I am a tackle junkie and still have most of the fly rods that I bought years ago, even though I keep threatening to have a yard sale to free up needed space. Before writing this section I took out of storage several of my favorite glass rods, now more than two decades old, on which I once caught large bluefish, bonefish, tarpon, amberjack, stripers, and a number of other species. I was not surprised to find that twenty years later, I could still throw the whole fly line with most of my glass rods. They are slower, and you do have to wait on them, but they will throw a line. Included in my glass-rod collection are rods by Fenwick, Browning/SilaFlex, Scientific Anglers, and Shakespeare. These glass rods had the same rating system (number 7, 9, 10, 11, etc.) that newer graphite rods have.

The first-generation graphite rods of the 1970s generated higher line speeds and were only a bit lighter than their glass counterparts. By the mid-1990s manufacturers were into the third and even fourth generation of graphite material and the resins that connect them. To say that rod building is now a high-tech art is an understatement. I own and use a variety of the best rods available on the market today, and I take great delight in them. There is, as you will quickly discover, a terrific price range in graphite saltwater rods. A good nine-foot rod for a 9-weight line can be bought for less than one hundred dollars, but it is also possible to pay five or six times that much for many of the top names and their latest casting tools.

Whether manufacturers describe their rods as having a "progressive taper" or a "fast tip with reserve power in the butt," modern graphite sticks generally have one thing in common: Saltwater rods are very quick and will generate significant line speed even without "hauling." Saltwater fly rods are not delicate, like spring creek trout rods. Wherever there are fish in salt water, there is wind, and fly fishermen must, whether they like it or not, be able to cast into the wind or crosswind. The higher line speeds developed by today's rods make penetrating the wind with big flies an easier proposition.

It would be foolish to say that any saltwater fly rod you buy is likely to be adequate. There is some junk out there. All fly rods are not created equal, and, to a certain degree, you do get what you pay for; but just exactly what are you getting? It is no coincidence that some of the top manufacturers of fly rods are located in the Pacific Northwest and other areas where graphite is used by the aerospace industry. Rod designers there and elsewhere are continuing to improve rod performance. When you buy an expensive, top-of-the-line rod from any manufacturer, you are buying the latest technology, best finishes, quality thread wraps, the highest-grade cork, and machined reel seats. By getting a medium-priced or lower-priced rod from a well-regarded company, you are usually getting an earlier-generation graphite blank with hardware and cork that will do the job but may not be as cosmetically pleasing. Although I love the top-of-the-line rods from such great companies as Sage, Loomis, Orvis, and Thomas & Thomas, I would be less than honest if I told you that you need their top-of-the-line rods for most conditions. Whether you are fishing for redfish near Charleston, large bluefish at Cape Hatteras, stripers off Martha's Vineyard, or sea trout behind Texas barrier islands, you do not need the latest and hottest equipment. If you are just beginning saltwater fly fishing, you may, for reasons of the pocketbook, want to get one of the "entry-level" rods available from the same name manufacturers. Many companies have complete entry level outfits with the rod, reel, and line for a very modest price. Almost any second-generation graphite will cast rings around the glass I used twenty-five years ago. If you develop good casting skills, you will find yourself able to fish with almost any serviceable fly rod. Remember, the rods that are now made from blanks of an earlier technology were touted just a few years ago as top of the line!

There is no perfect rod for all anglers. Early in this chapter, when I poked a little fun at people who test rods, I tried to make the point that the choice of action and feel is a very personal thing . . . a very subjective decision. Even though I can cast reasonably well with any good rod, I have found that I simply don't like the action of some rods, even some very expensive ones. I have also noticed that new fly rodders generally cast better with rods that are a little slower than the extremely fast actions found in some megabucks rods.

The most important thing to remember if you are new to the sport is that the outfit must be properly balanced. Balance simply means that you have a reel that is the right size and a line that is the proper weight for the fly rod you choose. If, for example, you try to use a 6-weight line on an 8-weight rod, you will find that the line is simply too light to flex the rod, or to load it. If, on the other hand, you try to use a number-12 line on an 8-weight rod, the problem will be just the opposite. The rod will simply be flexed beyond its limits to recover, making good casting almost impossible. Please keep in mind, however, that virtually all modern fly rods are capable of casting a line one weight below the suggested line weight for the rod and up to two line weights above. When I am using heavier flies, or fishing in windy conditions, I often use a number-10 line on a number-9 rod.

On several occasions I have cringed as I have watched non-fly-fishing salespeople in tackle shops or chain stores selling fly-fishing equipment about which they know little. I can think of no other sport where it is more important to deal with knowledgeable salespeople, either on the telephone or in person. Whether you are spending a few dollars or half a grand on a rod, take it for a "test drive" whenever possible. Fly-tackle shops should have a place where prospective purchasers can cast.

"If I Had Only One Rod"

I am asked the same question several dozen times each year: "If you could have only one fly rod for saltwater fly fishing, what would it be?" You can't play the game of golf with only one club, but in similar situations you can use the same club over and over again. The same is true of saltwater fly fishing. You should buy a rod that is matched both to the fish that you are most likely to seek and the conditions under which you will seek them. If most of your fishing is going to be for spotted weakfish and small red drum, then a nine-foot 8-weight rod will cover most situations. The same rod can be used for school stripers, Spanish mackerel, and bonefish. A good 8-weight rod can handle small- to medium-size flies and moderate wind conditions. If your main target is going to be larger striped bass in open water and big bluefish that like big flies, you will have to go to a 9- or 10-weight rod to cover your needs. On the Outer Banks of North Carolina there is almost always a wind problem and a variety of fish from which to choose. Since I may be using a small Clouser Minnow or a large popper, I have to use rods that give me a greater latitude, and a 9- or 10-weight rod provides it. If you plan on zeroing in on bigger fish, such as fall stripers in the New England surf, or fishing over wrecks for amberjack and cobia, you will want a rod that will throw large flies and also give you the ability to pressure large fish. For big critters you will want a number-11 or -12 rod.

At times when the winds are nil and the water clear, I enjoy catching Spanish mackerel, pompano, and even redfish on a 6- or a 7-weight rod. The average four- to six-pound redfish and any sea trout can be handled nicely on a 6- or 7-weight rod. When you add ten miles of wind, however, things begin to change quickly, and you will be reaching for your number 8.

No matter what rod you choose to begin your saltwater fly fishing, make sure it has enough "horsepower" for the fish you are going to tackle. False albacore can be hooked and landed on a number-6 rod . . . but most will die. False albacore and all mackerel should be fought hard and released quickly. If you do not use a rod that is substantial enough to bring fish in within a reasonable period of time, then "catch-and-release" will mean little. The same is true with striped bass and many other fish. I do not think it is a mark of a great fly fisherman to claim that he or she caught a fifteen-pound albacore or bluefish on a 5-weight rod. What that tells me is that the fish was unnecessarily stressed, when an 8, 9, or 10 outfit would have been a much better choice. So what's your perfect rod? It is a rod that is matched to the species and size of the fish you will be seeking, to the usual wind conditions, and to the size flies that you will be required to throw.

Saltwater fly rods usually come in two pieces, but most manufacturers now make available three- and four-piece travel rods. In earlier multipiece rods there were often dead spots at the ferrule. Bad multipiece rods are almost a thing of the past, and even the best casters are hard-pressed to tell the difference between a two-piece rod and a three- or four-piece rod. If you plan to travel—and travel is the name of the game in saltwater fly fishing—the multipiece rods sure pack easier. Virtually all of my "trip rods" are multipiece.

If you have to make a choice between putting most of your money into the rod or reel, invest more in the rod. It is the most important piece of equipment in the sport. Only a few fish require super reels. The most expensive rods are not always the best, but it is important to find a rod that is satisfying to you. A very subjective decision . . .

CHAPTER 8

REELS

Endless Choices for Every Fish and Wallet

In the early 1970s my first bonefish was caught on a Pflueger Medalist. When the big bluefish arrived on North Carolina's Outer Banks in the mid-seventies, the same Medalist, a model 1498, was just right for blues up to seventeen pounds. Because the reel had no counterbalance, there was major vibration and wobble anytime a fast fish took line or backing. The old-style caliper-foot drag was adequate but certainly not silky smooth, and the reel had no rim-control spool to make it easier to apply pressure. But the reel worked!

I still have my old Medalist and a substantial collection of saltwater fly reels from a number of manufacturers. I have top-of-the-line reels as well as some of the lower-priced offerings. My earliest quality reels came from Fin-Nor, Seamaster, John Emery, and Ted Juracsik (Billy Pate models). These reels literally opened fly-fishing horizons to all fish and all oceans. More recently, other top-of-the-line reels have come on the market from producers such as Able, Lamson, Islander, Orvis, Ross, and Penn. I love fine workmanship and the close tolerances of the great reels. As with any tool, however, you pay for quality. What many new fly rodders don't understand is that the vast majority of fish sought by fly rodders, especially on the East and Gulf coasts, do not require a machined spool, large line capacity, and whisper-smooth drag.

I am afraid that some anglers may have actually stayed away from fly fishing because of a perceived high price tag for entry. There are now plenty of fly reels on the market in all price ranges to match the needs and wallet size of any angler. Many of the manufacturers I just mentioned offer a second tier of excellent reels for salt water at a fraction of the cost of their best reels. Other manufacturers, including Scientific Anglers, Martin, Valentine, and STH, offer good value for the money.

Teenagers often believe they cannot play basketball without a hundred-dollar pair of "Super Air Pumps" worn by major college and NBA players, and some fly rodders purchase high-priced reels because they are convinced that nothing else will do the job. I plead guilty to having played the expensive "tennis-shoe game" with fly reels. A couple of years ago two friends and I were fishing for spotted weakfish and

Almost all top-of-the-line saltwater fly reels have a large circular disc that presses directly against the spool (see exposed disc of center reel). Four of the top reels on the market include the Islander (top left), Lamson Saltwater Series (top right), Abel (bottom left), and Orvis Odyssey (bottom right). Photograph by Tom Earnhardt

Many of the best medium priced fly reels offer drags that press on a metal disc, or plate, that is separate from the spool itself. Such drag systems are more than adequate for most inshore fish. Three popular reels include the Orvis DXR (top row), Lamson LP (middle row), and the Scientific Anglers Two (bottom row). Photograph by Tom Earnhardt

There are a number of relatively inexpensive fly reels suitable for a wide variety of inshore fish. Included in this category are reels by Orvis (top left), Ross (top right), Scientific Anglers (bottom left), and Pflueger (bottom right).
Photograph by Tom Earnhardt

puppy drum in a tidal marsh studded with oyster bars. It was about noon when we noticed that the three reels in use were five-hundred-dollar tarpon-class models. We began laughing when we compared the tackle we were using with the low speed and lightweight quarry we were seeking. The biggest weakfish we caught that day was about three pounds, and the largest redfish probably seven. No elephant guns needed there. . . .

If you want the best available, or if you are pursuing fast, large fish, then by all means buy a top-drawer reel. The great reels will last a lifetime and are just nice to hold. Price, however, should not be an obstacle for someone wanting to pursue most saltwater fish.

REEL FEATURES TO CONSIDER

The first consideration for new anglers is whether to purchase a direct drive or an antireverse reel. The direct drives are popular among saltwater anglers because there are a greater number of models available and because most experienced anglers like the contact with fish that direct drives allow. The essential difference between a direct drive and an antireverse is that the handle of an antireverse reel does not spin

There are a number of specialty fly reels on the market for saltwater use. Valentine (top left) and Abel (top right) make antireverse reels. The direct-drive Loop reel with its large-diameter spool allows anglers to pick up line much faster than with conventional saltwater reels.
Photograph by Tom Earnhardt

when a fish runs. Because the handle is stationary while the spool of the reel moves, anglers using an antireverse do not have to worry about getting their fingernails or knuckles cracked by a fast-revolving handle. The main disadvantage of antireverse reels is that a turn of the handle does not always mean line is being recovered, resulting in less control of the pressure being put on a fish. The choice of direct drive or antireverse, however, is, like so many other things in angling, a matter of preference. While experienced anglers tend to prefer direct drives, some of the very best, like Billy Pate, have taken more large fish than most of us can imagine on antireverse reels. For the record I own both styles but use direct drives.

Although a few companies offer multiplying fly reels for saltwater fly fishing with a two-to-one or greater retrieve ratio, I don't know many anglers who use them. Such reels allow you to gather loose line off a deck faster and to get back line more quickly during the fight. One of the beauties of fly fishing is its simplicity. Most fly rodders prefer a one-to-one ratio and gladly give up many of the advantages, such as a higher-speed line retrieve, found in other fishing techniques. In order to maintain the traditional one-to-one retrieve ratio, while at the same time allowing for a faster retrieve, a number of manufacturers have made reels with narrower, large-diameter spools that pick up line much faster than smaller-diameter spools. One manufacturer,

Loop of Sweden, makes quality reels with extremely large spools. Don't let convention stand in your way. If your hand gets cramped using the slower pickup of traditional reels, then get a multiplier and enjoy it!

When choosing a fly reel, you should consider a number of other things, as well. The reel should, above all, be matched to the rod and fly line you intend to use. A reel that is much too small or large for a given rod will not balance well. Also, if the reel is too small, you may not be able to get much backing on it in addition to the fly line required for the rod. For example, if you use a reel more suited for a 6- or 7-weight line on a rod with a number-9 designation, you will be lucky to get a 9-weight line on the reel with any backing at all. Although balance is important, you should also make sure that the reel you choose is properly matched to your target species. For example, when fishing for weakfish, school stripers, small red drum, or Spanish mackerel, reels with a hundred yards of backing will do just fine. However, when fishing for long-running species, such as false albacore, a reel that holds at least two hundred yards of backing is a far better choice. Again, choose a reel that is balanced to the rod and to the species you target.

LEFT OR RIGHT

Probably no topic related to the choice of reels elicits more heated discussion than whether an angler should choose a left-hand-wind or right-hand-wind fly reel. Right-handed casters traditionally use their right hand to hold the rod during the cast. When the fish is played, however, the rod is held in the left hand and the reel handle is turned with the fingers of the right hand. Traditional left-handers follow the same sequence, just reversed. This means that your dominant hand is operating the reel while your weaker hand is holding the rod and fighting the fish. Even though there is no right way or wrong way, I have made an informal eyeball survey over the past few years. I have noted that close to half of the right-handed anglers I have observed, and especially those new to the sport, use a left-hand-retrieve reel.

I am right-handed and own reels for both left- and right-hand retrieve, but my clear preference has been to use left-hand-retrieve reels, especially for larger, long-fighting fish. Although I attempt to make no converts, here's why left-hand retrieve is more comfortable and practical for me. First, my right arm is my dominant arm and therefore stronger. When I cast with my right arm, I see no reason to transfer the rod from right hand to left in order to play a fish. I am able to pick up line very fast and do not buy the argument that one can turn a reel significantly faster with his or her dominant hand. Many new saltwater fly fishermen come from a spin-fishing background. The vast majority of right-handed spin fishermen cast with their right hand and retrieve with their left hand. To such anglers the use of the left-hand-wind reel is often easier.

I am completely aware that most conventional reels (bait casting) require the angler to cast with the right hand, pass the rod to the left hand, and then wind with the right. I am also aware that most trolling rods are wound with the right hand while the rod is pumped with the left. The bottom line for fly fishermen, whether left- or right-handed, is to choose a fly reel with the handle on the side that is most comfortable. Faster retrieve speeds can be developed in time with either hand. Whichever way you choose, I can assure you that you are in good company. Flip Pallot of "Walker's Cay Chronicles," a right-handed caster, branded me a "wrong-handed" fly fisherman when he saw me using a left-hand-wind reel. Flip, Lefty Kreh, and many other right-handers are part of the right-hand-wind school. The late Lee Wulff was an advocate of left-hand wind for righties. John Harder, president of Lamson Reels, is a right-hand caster who also likes to play strong fish with his right hand. Like me, John believes that "left-hand wind is right." The debate goes on. . . .

Drags

Another source of confusion for those new to saltwater fly fishing is the choice of drags. Every manufacturer of saltwater fly reels claims to have a smooth, durable drag, and, fortunately, most are telling the truth. The job for the consumer/angler is to choose the drag type that is best suited to his or her angling needs. The drags found on most expensive fly reels share one common characteristic: They all have a relatively large-diameter cork, or cork/composite, drag surface on a plate, or disc, that presses directly against the spool as the drag is tightened. These are sometimes referred to as ratchet-and-pawl systems. Such drags can handle the punishment offered by any fish. The top-of-the-line reels from manufacturers such as Abel, Billy Pate, Penn, Lamson, Fin-Nor, Sea Master, Orvis, and others all use large circular discs that press directly against the spool. Such drags not only slow down fish, but they also tend to last forever. I have several Fin-Nor "wedding cake" reels and a couple of Sea Masters that have worked perfectly for over twenty years with no repair work on the drags.

Most of the value-priced and medium-priced fly reels are also billed as having disc drags. Most of the disc drags found on these reels involve the use of calipers (Scientific Anglers, System II, and Lamson, LP Series) faced with heat-resistant material against a metal plate, or disc, that is separate from the spool itself. Other manufacturers use a full circle (Orvis, DXR series) of high-tech facing, which is pressed against a separate metal disc. Even though these disc drags offer much less drag surface than the more expensive cork/composite "against-the-spool" systems, they do a very good job. Since reels with a separate offset disc system often cost as little as one-third of the disc-against-spool models, they are a good choice for anglers seeking all but the largest, fastest gamefish. For spotted weakfish, red drum, stripers, false albacore, bonito, bluefish, and even tarpon, these reels will do the job. With care they will last many years. I use several of these lower-cost, lighter-weight reels and believe that they are good reels, not just a compromise.

A few saltwater reels are available with the old click-and-pawl drag system. The click-and-pawl, found on many freshwater fly reels, is the least expensive of all systems and is intended to stop overrun of the fly reel and to produce a relatively small amount of drag. Since drag pressure can also be added by palming the spool and by putting pressure on the fly line with your fingers, a click-and-pawl is satisfactory for many smaller, slower critters in the ocean. Even top manufacturers like Abel offer click-and-pawl models for use in the salt.

Several companies (Ross and Charlton) offer reels with large sealed shafts running through the spool. Drag resistance is generated by pressure on sandwiches of discs and other components inside the shaft. Reels with this system can be moderate to expensive in price.

Earlier, I mentioned "palming" the spool as an additional braking technique. Virtually all direct-drive saltwater fly reels on the market, whether they have a machined spool or a cast-metal spool, have an exposed or overlapping rim. Some of the best antireverse reels also have a palming rim. When a fish is running, an overlapping spool rim gives the angler the option of applying additional pressure simply by putting his or her palm against the spool. In the case of a hot-running fish, a piece of shirt can be held against the spool rim to keep hands from being burned. For the few reels that do not have overlapping spool rims, the angler can place a finger behind and against the line or backing to provide additional drag.

All fly reels, regardless of price, should have a small weight or counterbalance on the opposite side of the spool from the handle. For slow-speed fish a counterbalance is not that important; but when a false albacore strips off 150 yards at high speed, a counterbalance stops the wobble. Some of the new top-of-the-line reels, such as the Islander series, have put counterweights on both sides of the spool to prevent wobble.

FINISH AND CONSTRUCTION

An important factor worthy of consideration, and often a difference in the price breakpoint in reels, is whether the reel is anodized or enameled. Most of the top-of-the-line reels come with either gold, black, or black-and-gold anodized finishes. Many are highly polished, but some have an anodized matte finish. These finishes are made to resist saltwater corrosion and extend the life of the reel. Virtually all of the anodized spools and frames are machined from high-grade aluminum alloy. The fact that spools and frames are cut from one piece of metal greatly adds to the cost of the final product. Reels that are made of cast metal (poured into molds) are generally much less expensive. Such reels are usually protected with an enamel finish, polyurethane epoxy, or a smooth Teflon coating. Cast-metal spools are, as a rule, not as strong as the spools machined out of bar-stock alloy, but plenty tough for saltwater middleweights.

All reels need to be cleaned after use in salt water, and this is especially true of those reels that are coated with an enamel or Teflon finish. Even the smallest chip can start the corrosion process. Anodized reels also need to be cleaned, although the finish is part of the metal itself. My usual routine after a couple of days on the water is to wash all fly reels with a solution of mild, soapy water followed by a good freshwater rinse. Springs, bearings, and other moving parts usually get a small amount of oil.

When discussing fly-reel construction it is important to know what backing is suited to the reel. Some types of backing simply cannot be used on saltwater fly reels. Monofilament is not an acceptable backing for most, although there are some exceptions. Monofilament will stretch significantly when pulled off the reel by a fast-running fish. When packed back onto the spool, stretched monofilament can cause tremendous pressure to build up—pressure that can literally blow out the sides of most spools. The most accepted and used backing is Dacron or Cortland's Micron in twenty- or thirty-pound test. More on backing later . . .

There is little question that high-quality reels with machined spools and anodized finishes are the premier reels made for saltwater fly fishing. Their oversize disc-against-spool drags can last for a lifetime of fishing. Some have glossy finishes that should be the envy of any sports-car buff. For all these qualities you pay extra, and if you can afford it, it's probably worth it.

As indicated previously, however, there are plenty of reels for most fish and pocketbooks that will allow price-conscious anglers to enjoy the sport. Most of us do not buy cars or shoes that last a lifetime, nor should we expect the same of most fly reels. The choices have never been as good as they are today, so there is no excuse for not finding a quality reel that will get you in the game.

CHAPTER 9

LINES AND LEADERS
No, Not More Knots!

For those new to the sport of saltwater fly fishing, there is no more confusing area than the selection of lines and leaders and the choice of knots. Look at any major fly-fishing catalog or walk into any tackle shop, and you'll know what I mean. There are level lines, double tapers, long-belly weight forwards, saltwater tapers, shooting heads, tropic tapers, bass tapers, and billfish tapers. Just when you've digested that, you'll find out that there are floaters, intermediate sinkers, five-foot sink tips, ten-foot sink tips, twenty-foot sink tips, thirty-foot sinking shooting heads, and full sinkers; and don't forget different densities that sink to different levels! Add to all of these the choice of colors—chartreuse, mint green, olive, buckskin, sunrise, orange, sand, pale yellow, ivory, and clear—and you may be approaching a condition known as "fly-line breakdown."

I have a closetfull of fly lines, and I am really not complaining, because Scientific Anglers, Cortland, Orvis, L. L. Bean, Jim Teeny, and several other producers and distributors of fly lines have met every conceivable need of the saltwater fly fisherman. There are literally hundreds of styles, types, and sizes of lines available at prices—sometimes over fifty dollars a line—that give "sticker shock" a new meaning. One friend put it to me this way: "I had just gotten over the fact that the fly rod and reel you'd suggested were equal to my monthly mortgage payment, when on top of that the clerk added a car payment—in the form of three fly lines and a handful of leader spools."

The truth is that to optimize your chances at success in saltwater fly fishing, you often need to carry several different lines with you at any given time. What is not necessary for most anglers, however, is a large number of "specialty" lines, which only *marginally* increase your chances for success. When thinking about what fly lines to take on a trip, I try to make sure that I answer these questions: Do the lines I am taking match up with my rods (i.e., an 8- or 9-weight line for an 8-weight rod)? Are the lines appropriate for the water conditions I intend to fish (i.e., shallow flats or rough surf)? Finally, what is the likelihood that I will be presenting flies to fish in deeper waters or in fast currents?

Without hesitation I can say that at least 95 percent of all my fly fishing can be done with three lines. The 5 percent "fudge factor" covers those times when I want to use one of many specialty lines. In the Mid-Atlantic region and along the Gulf Coast, fully 50 percent of all of my fly fishing is with a floating line. With floating lines I have taken just about every shallow-water feeder and surface feeder available to fly rodders—including cobia, redfish, sea trout, flounder, Spanish mackerel, king mackerel, false albacore, bonito, bluefish, jack crevalle, and dolphin. A floating line matched to your rod is the center of your fly-fishing arsenal.

I am not trying to be evasive when I tell you that there are great floating lines available from all of the quality line suppliers and manufacturers. Among my favorites are the Mastery floating lines from Scientific Anglers, the Cortland 444SL series, and the Orvis HLS series of lines. For the East and Gulf coasts—for any coast, for that matter—I do not believe it is necessary to use the "extra-stiff" saltwater floating lines (made with braided nylon core) or lines with extremely short tapers or extremely long tapers. A good all-around floating fly line will meet most of your fishing needs. I have caught lots of tarpon, for example, on standard-weight forward floaters, even though "tarpon" tapers may be marginally better.

The next line most likely to be used by most fly fishermen is the intermediate, or slow-sinking, fly line. Intermediate lines sink below the surface very slowly and are a favorite line for surf and flats. Intermediate lines, built in a weight-forward configuration, are great casting lines, especially in windy conditions. Because they are a little more dense than a floating line, and have a smaller profile, intermediates cut through a stiff breeze extremely well. Slow sinkers can be used almost everywhere you can use a floating line, but there is one place where the intermediate line is distinctly better. When fishing light surf, I always choose an intermediate line over a floating line. Rolling waves will invariably have a more drastic effect on a floating line than an intermediate. Being on the surface, a floating line is much more likely to be treated like flotsam and tossed by the waves, whereas an intermediate will go through and under the waves. Most major manufacturers provide intermediate lines, and all have excellent shooting qualities.

The third type of line, which I find myself using probably 20 percent of the time, is the high-speed Sink-Tip or sinking head that helps take your fly down in deeper water and keeps it down in fast currents. As I indicated earlier, there are some people who believe that fly fishing is a surface sport and don't like "dredging" with sinking fly lines. I respect anyone with this view; however, such fishermen are missing out on a lot of great saltwater opportunities that a high-density Sink-Tip/head line can open to them. Sink-Tips, or heads, are simply faster-sinking sections (ten to thirty-five feet in length) followed by sixty to eighty feet of small-diameter running line. I find these lines useful when fishing in deeper water for weakfish, large red drum, stripers, blues, and many of the wreck species that are reluctant to come to the surface. My largest dolphin over the years have been caught on sinking heads, which took my fly underneath smaller "shingle" dolphin on the surface. If tarpon are to be caught consistently in the waters of Virginia, the Carolinas, or Georgia, I am convinced that the use of sinking heads is the method that will prove successful.

If you want a sinking line for every condition, you might want to use a shooting-head system that allows you to loop shooting heads of various densities into a single running line. I have found that most of my deep-water or heavy-surf fishing can be done with a Sink-Tip/head twenty-four to thirty feet in length with a permanently attached running line. A head weight of 400 to 450 grains can be used on a 9- to 12-weight rod and can easily handle a wide variety of conditions. My favorites are the Jim Teeny lines, the T400, and the TS450, but Cortland's twenty-four-foot Quick Sink and L. L. Bean's Superhead connection-free sinking heads are also excellent. Again, it is easy to accumulate a large number of sinking and Sink-Tip lines that *you will rarely use.* The trick is to find one line that will work on several rods. With the three types of line already mentioned, a weight forward floating, an intermediate, and a twenty-four- to thirty-foot Sink-Tip/head line, you will be prepared for success in any waters.

There are a few situations found in every fishery that will call for a very specialized line, such as a high-speed full sinking line or a shooting head with monofilament running line. Also keep in mind that each type of fly line, from floating to sinking head, has different casting characteristics, which will be dealt with in chapter 12. Finally, if you do carry two or three different fly lines, it is not necessary to own several reels or even extra spools, since there are ways to change fly lines quickly in the field. These quick-change methods will be addressed later in this chapter.

All new lines and lines that have been stored on the reel, even overnight, should be stretched before use. Before I begin casting I always stretch lines to avoid frustration, tangles, and lost fish. Kinky flylines never cast well.

BACKING

One of the things that separates most freshwater fly fishing from the salty variety is the need for larger reels and backing. The fly lines just discussed are only part of the system of leaders and knots between angler and fish. Fly rodders should look at the knot connecting the backing to the reel all the way to the knot connecting the fly to the tippet, and everything in between, as a continuum. This system, made up of backing, fly line, and leader, is only as good as the materials used and the knots that hold it all together.

For almost the entire time I have fished in salt water, I have used either twenty-pound- or thirty-pound-test Dacron or Cortland's Micron backing. For smaller- to medium-weight fish such as weakfish, redfish, bonefish, and bonito, I almost always use twenty-pound-test backing. Some fish, such as weakfish and Spanish mackerel, require almost no backing, where others, such as false albacore and bonito, will call for a minimum of two hundred yards of backing behind your fly line.

Although the teeth of a bonito look formidable, they are not cutting teeth. For bonito a standard saltwater leader with a tippet testing ten to twelve pounds is all that is necessary.
Photograph by Captain Mike Kenfield

Captain Tommy Gunn shows the business end of a North Carolina barracuda. Wire tippets must be used for barracuda, king mackerel, and sharks.
Photograph by Joel Arrington

For heavier fish and for larger rods (10 weight and above), I normally use thirty-pound-test backing. When fishing for tarpon, amberjack, cobia, or even large stripers, anglers will often use a sixteen-pound-test leader or, in some cases, even an IGFA twenty-pound-class leader. When using a heavy leader, you do not want to use a backing with a breaking strength close to that of the leader. It would be foolish to use a twenty-pound-test backing and a twenty-pound-test class tippet since failure of the backing would mean the loss of not only the fish but the entire fly line. Most of the smaller fish I've mentioned—bonito, redfish, and bonefish—rarely call for a tippet testing more than twelve pounds, making a twenty-pound-test backing appropriate.

You will note that I emphasized Dacron as my choice of backing. Braided Dacron and its very close cousin, Cortland's Micron, are relatively small in diameter, and have a small amount of stretch when compared to monofilament. Both have excellent knot strength and normally have a long life before needing replacement. Virtually all salt-water-reel manufacturers give the backing capacity of their reels in either twenty-pound or thirty-pound braided Dacron. Other types of backing can actually damage or destroy many saltwater fly reels. Very few saltwater fly reels can be used with monofilament backing, because all monofilaments stretch much more than braided Dacron or Micron. When a fish makes a long run, monofilament, when wound back on the reel, will produce tremendous internal pressures against the inside of the reel's spool. The spools of even very good reels can be pushed out like a doughnut or even cracked by too much interior pressure. Aside from the possibility of damage to the reel, monofilament, with all of its stretch, does not give the angler the same control over a long-running fish as does a braided Dacron or Micron backing.

In recent years some new "super backings" (gel-spun polyethylene and polyethylene variations) have appeared on the market. They are advertised as high-strength, small-diameter, low-stretch backings. Anglers can often put twice as much of these new backings (with a higher breaking strength) on a spool than is possible with Dacron or Micron. I have used some of these new backings and find them totally unnecessary for virtually all saltwater fly fishing done on the East and Gulf coasts. First, with very small diameters, it is much more likely that an angler can get a serious line cut. Perhaps as significant, however, are the very high prices being sought for the new high-strength, tiny-diameter backings. The new backings cost significantly more than a comparable length of Dacron or Micron. However, for large billfish, and for speedsters such as wahoo and yellowfin tuna, there is a place for these new lines, because they greatly increase reel capacity and offer less resistance while being pulled through the water.

KNOTS

Beginning with the connection of backing to your fly reel, knots are everything. One bad knot can cause the entire system to fail. Like the selection of fly lines mentioned earlier, there is a dizzying array of knot choices for almost every job confronting the angler. You will find drawings of knots on fly-line boxes, on the back of leader packets, and in magazines. In several excellent fly-fishing books, including Lou Tabory's *Inshore Fly Fishing*, Lefty Kreh's *Fly Fishing in Salt Water*, and, more specifically, Lefty Kreh and Mark Sosin's *Practical Fishing Knots II*, you will find superb drawings and advice. Rather than trying to reinvent the wheel by going through all the possible options, I have decided to include only the one or two knots that I have found most useful in each situation. Knot tying is an art and an integral part of any fly fisherman's education, but it is necessary to master only a few basic knots to get a full measure of enjoyment from the sport. Tying good knots is not difficult, and once you have learned, you will become reluctant to allow anyone, even your guides, to tie knots for you.

The first thing to remember about knots is that, with few exceptions, almost all knots decrease the strength of the backing, fly line, or leader material. The object is therefore to choose knots that when properly tied diminish line strength as little as possible. The first knot you will have to tie is the one attaching the backing to the fly reel. The knot most often used for this purpose is the Arbor Knot (not shown).

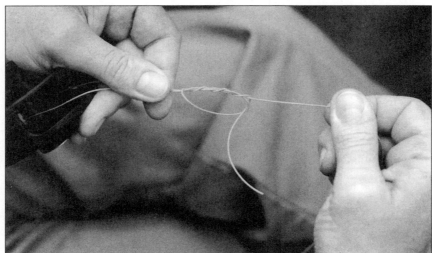

DUNCAN LOOP The Duncan Loop, also known as the Uni-Knot, is one of the best knots for attaching backing to a fly-reel spool. Four turns are sufficient for attaching backing to the spool.

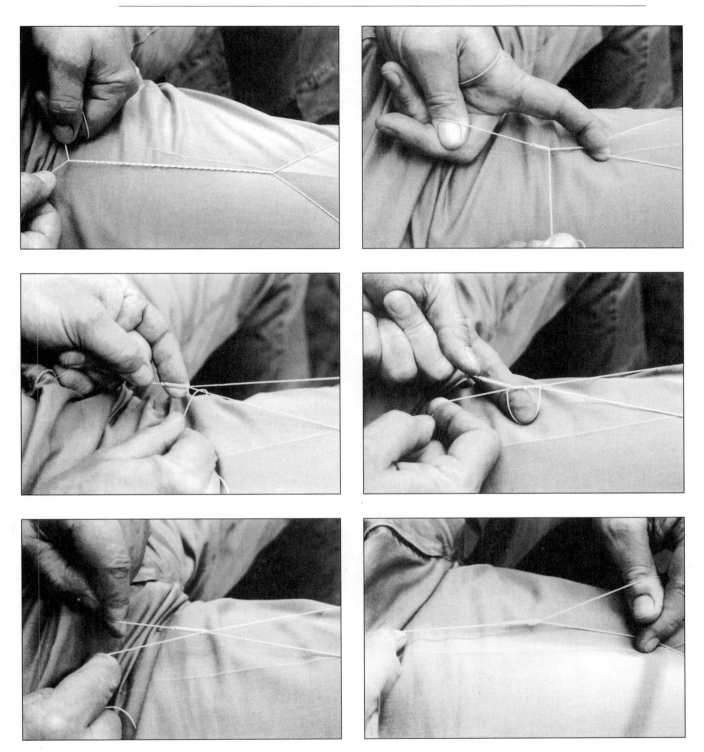

BIMINI TWIST *One of the most important knots a fly fisherman can learn is a Bimini Twist, also known as a Twenty Turn Knot. This is a hundred percent knot which is used in several places in the saltwater fly fisherman's knot system. First, it is an excellent way of putting a large loop in the backing where the fly line and backing are joined together. Second, it is the best knot to use for the construction of big-game leaders to insure that the breaking strength of the tippet will not be diminished at the knot.*

Although it looks difficult, the Bimini Twist is not a difficult knot to tie. The only part that some anglers find difficult is the phase where the index finger of one hand is pulled into the fork of the loop, creating tension in the Twenty Turn below it. By applying firm pressure with the index finger, anglers should be able to lay twenty smooth turns to the point where the tag end and fork in the loop come together. A simple Half Hitch will hold the twenty turns in place until the knot can be completed as shown.

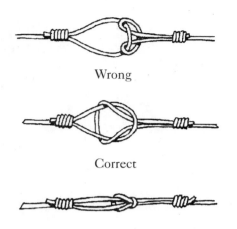

Wrong

Correct

LOOP TO LOOP The Loop to Loop connection is the way to lock loops together properly. Leaders can be changed quickly with interlocking loops.

Another knot that can be used in this situation, and my choice, is a four-turn Duncan loop, also known as a Uni-Knot (see page 68). No knot at the fly reel will keep your line from breaking if a fish has already taken all of your fly line and all of your backing. If a running fish has got you to this point, you are in big trouble.

At the other end of the backing, where it joins the fly line, I always create a loop. I use a Bimini Twist, one of the most important knots a fly fisherman can know (see page 69). The Bimini Twist is also an integral part of "big-game leader" construction, which will be shown later. Where the backing joins the fly line, I tie a Bimini Twist so that there is an open loop fifteen to eighteen inches in length. Because you will have put a small loop at the end of the fly line (to be illustrated later), you can then use a Figure Eight loop-to-loop connection (see diagram). With a Bimini Twist loop at the end of your backing, you will be able to change fly lines quickly provided that you have already put small loops in the ends of your extra fly lines. In an emergency, or if you are simply unable to master the tying of the Bimini Twist, you can also put the loop in your backing with a Surgeon's Loop (see page 71), or with a knot known as the Spider Hitch (not shown).

The short loop in the reel end of your fly line can be constructed in several ways, but by far the best way I have found is the loop called a Bobbin Whip Loop. Note that the loop, approximately an inch and a half in length, is formed by wrapping nylon thread over the end of the fly line, which has been rolled back over on itself (see page 72). The first thing I do when I buy a new fly line is to put a loop in it. The loop in the fly-line, along with the larger loop in the Bimini Twist at the end of the backing, allows me to change fly lines quickly and easily. The large loop at the end of the backing allows me to pass an entire fly-line container or fly reel through the loop when changing lines.

At the business end, or forward end, of the fly line, you will also need a loop. Some people actually put a very small loop in the end of the fly line and then Figure Eight their leader directly to the fly line. For a number of years, however, I have preferred a permanent butt section of monofilament leader material at the end of my fly line, with a loop in the end of the monofilament butt section. For the permanent butt section used with "standard saltwater leaders" (described later) I use eighteen inches to two feet of neither very limp nor extra-hard monofilament. My favorite leader material for the permanent butt section is made by Maxima, a material of moderate stiffness and larger than average diameter. For standard leaders on 7- through 9-weight lines I use a thirty-pound-test permanent butt, and on 10- or 11-weight lines, a forty-pound-test permanent butt section. For "big-game leaders," to be discussed later, I use a hard monofilament butt section three or four feet in length.

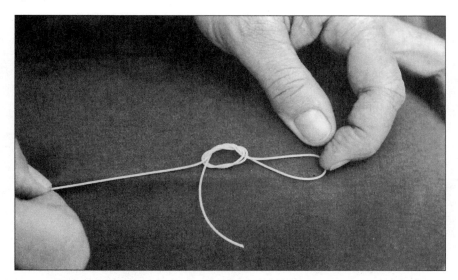

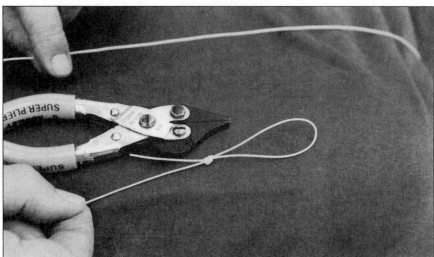

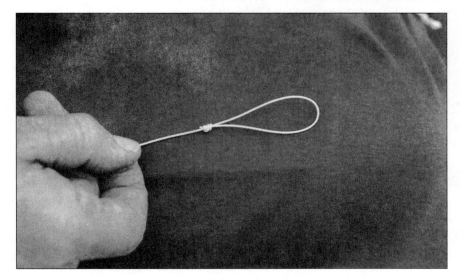

SURGEON'S LOOP If you choose not to use the Duncan Loop to put a loop in the end of your permanent butt section, then use a Surgeon's Loop. The Surgeon's Loop is an easy-to-tie, non-slip knot that works very well, especially with monofilament testing less than twenty pounds. It's only disadvantage is that it does not have the small profile of the Duncan Loop when used with monofilament testing thirty pounds or greater.

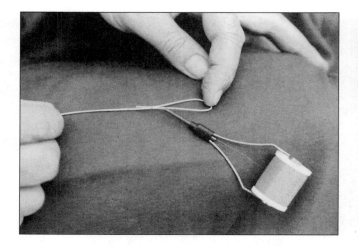

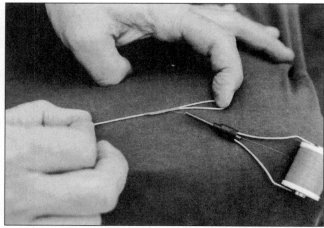

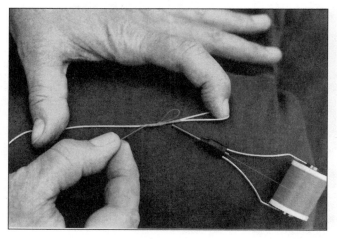

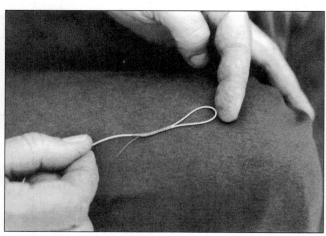

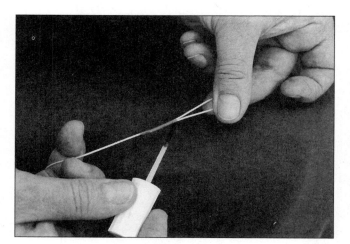

BOBBIN WHIP LOOP The Bobbin Whip Loop is a terrific way of putting a short permanent loop in the end of the fly line where it is attached to the backing. Before beginning this knot it is best to cut the end of the fly line at a 45-degree angle. The sharp point created by cutting the fly line at an angle allows one to tie a smoother Bobbin Whip Loop.

Using a fly-tying bobbin and nylon-tying thread, form a short loop by wrapping over the doubled fly line. After completing the wrapping process and securing the thread as shown in the diagram, paint over the nylon thread with nail polish or fly-tying head cement.

The monofilament must be connected to the fly line, and there is no better way than with a Nail Knot (see page 73). There are two ways to tie a Nail Knot, but I have chosen to show only the standard Nail Knot as opposed to the Speed Nail Knot. The Nail Knot is a must knot for fly fishermen. It can also be used to attach your backing to the end of your fly line if you do not desire to have a quick-change large loop, as shown earlier.

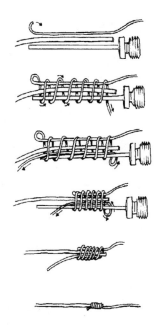

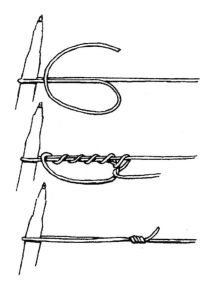

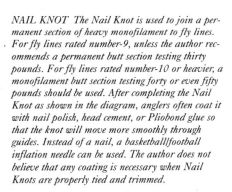

NAIL KNOT The Nail Knot is used to join a permanent section of heavy monofilament to fly lines. For fly lines rated number-9, unless the author recommends a permanent butt section testing thirty pounds. For fly lines rated number-10 or heavier, a monofilament butt section testing forty or even fifty pounds should be used. After completing the Nail Knot as shown in the diagram, anglers often coat it with nail polish, head cement, or Pliobond glue so that the knot will move more smoothly through guides. Instead of a nail, a basketball/football inflation needle can be used. The author does not believe that any coating is necessary when Nail Knots are properly tied and trimmed.

DUNCAN LOOP A Duncan Loop, using five turns, is an excellent way to put a loop in the permanent monofilament butt section at the end of the fly line or in the butt section of a leader. The loops, about one inch in length, can be formed by putting them over a stationary object such as a nail or the end of a boat cleat and then pulling hard on the tag end. The author recommends that loops tied with this knot should be used only with monofilament testing thirty pounds or more.

After attaching your butt-section material to your fly line with a Nail Knot, you will want to tie a loop in the end of your monofilament butt section. The two knots that I favor are the Surgeon's Loop (see page 71) and the Duncan Loop/Uni-Knot (see page 68). I admit that more fishermen probably use the Surgeon's Loop, which is an excellent knot and does not slip. However, I believe that when properly tied, a five-turn Duncan Loop does a superior job. You will probably note that the Duncan Loop is a slipknot, but when two sections of relatively large-diameter (thirty- to fifty-pound-test) monofilament are looped together using a Figure Eight connection, the Duncan Loops will not slip. I have caught many large tarpon, cobia, and amberjack and never had the five-turn Duncan Loop fail. Although the Double Surgeon's Loop is a great knot, the Duncan Loop offers a smaller profile. Another popular knot for making a loop is the Nonslip Mono Loop (not shown)—a good knot, but not my preference.

BUILDING A LEADER

The permanent butt section loop is the place you will attach your leader, and for salt-water use you will need two basic types. The first type is the "standard saltwater leader," eight to twelve feet in length. This is one most often used for the vast major-ity of smaller and medium-size fish. If you really want to keep it simple, you can buy them premade and knotless in a variety of lengths (seven and a half to twelve feet) and tippet strengths. Most tackle shops and fly-fishing catalogs will offer a number of choices. Again, I would caution you not to get an extremely limp or a very stiff leader if you buy the premade ones. Knotless nine-foot leaders are a good choice for most surface and near-surface fishing.

I almost always use my own hand-tied leaders, but whether I'm using hand-tied or knotless leaders in salt water, I always put my own loop in the heavy monofilament butt of the leader. As with the permanent butt loop at the end of my fly line, I pre-fer a five-turn Duncan Loop or a Surgeon's Loop in the heavy section of my leader. The loop in the permanent butt section and the loop in the heavy butt section of your leader should be made of material that is approximately the same diameter and test strength.

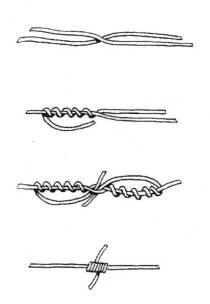

BLOOD KNOT The Blood Knot is used to tie sections of monofilament together that are similar in size and breaking strength. By graduating monofilament sizes from larger to smaller (30-pound test to 20, 20-pound test to 15, 15-pound test to 12, etc., as discussed in text), anglers can build their own standard leaders using the Nail Knot. When tying larger-test monofilament together, use a Nail Knot with only four or five turns on each side. With smaller-diameter monofilament (16-pound test and less) six to eight turns should be used on each of the knots.

If you don't choose ready-made knotless tapered leaders, you will find that it is very easy to make your own high-quality leaders in the exact length and stiffness you desire. I have seen many "formulas" in magazine articles and books for the construction of leaders. When you break them down, they almost always fall into either what Lefty Kreh and Mark Sosin call the 60-20-20 method, or the 50-30-30 formula preferred by other experts. All this means is that 50 or 60 percent of your leader should be of heavier butt material, 20 or 30 percent should be medium-diameter "hinge" material, and the last 20 percent of your leader should be lighter "tippet" material. Each section of the leader is attached to the previous section with a Blood Knot (see diagram).

For example, a well-constructed twelve-foot leader, good for redfish, sea trout, Spanish macker-el, false albacore, school stripers, and a variety of other inshore fish, should be built as follows: The butt section of your standard saltwater leader should start with a three-foot section of thirty-pound test Blood Knotted to a three-foot section of twenty-five-pound test. The midsection, or "hinge," should be made up of a one-foot section of twenty-pound test, Blood Knotted to a one-foot piece of sixteen-pound test. To make a leader with a twelve-pound tippet, simply Blood Knot an addi-

IMPROVED CLINCH KNOT The Improved Clinch Knot is used for tying smaller-diameter monofila-ment directly to the fly. Again, depending on the size of the monofilament, six to eight turns should be used.

tional two feet of twelve-pound-test material to the sixteen-pound-test end of the
hinge section. Leaders of different lengths
can be tied by varying the length of each
section of monofilament, according to the
formulas. I know of a number of excellent
fly rodders who fish with very simple leaders tied with only three sections of
monofilament. For a nine-foot leader they
use three feet of twenty-five-pound test,
three feet of sixteen, and three feet of
twelve Blood Knotted together. A loop is
put in the twenty-five-pound section and

*The Improved Blood Knot is identical to the reg-
ular Blood Knot except that one side of the knot
is tied with a double line. This is a very practical
knot for joining smaller-diameter shock tippets
directly to the test tippet. The author recommends
using twenty-five to thirty-pound-test monofilament shock tippets when fishing for medium-sized
stripers and redfish.*

looped to the permanent thirty-pound butt section. This simple 3-3-3 leader may not
turn over as well as the more complex leaders but will do the job for sea trout, redfish, and small stripers. You can tie leaders at home on wintry afternoons, or on an air-
plane. The finished leaders, with a loop in the butt section, should be coiled and
stored in a small plastic sandwich bag and marked both as to butt-section test and tippet test. Store them away from light and heat, and they should be good for several
years.

With the standard leader your fly should be tied to the tippet with an Improved
Clinch Knot (see page 75). This is one of many knots used to tie monofilament to
the eye of the hook, and one of the best. It should be noted that standard leaders can
be modified to add a light monofilament shock tippet or a short piece of wire. If you
are going to be fishing for ladyfish, jack crevalle, or medium-size stripers, you will
want a foot or less of thirty-pound test. This light "shock tippet" can be attached to
the test tippet with an Improved Blood Knot (see diagram). For bluefish and other
smaller toothy critters use a short trace, eight inches or less, of twenty- to forty-pound
coated wire. The test tippet and wire are joined with an Albright Knot (see page 78).

Finally, if you are fishing with a Sink-Tip, sinking head, or full sinking line, a *very
short* leader is far superior. An eight- to twelve-foot leader will allow the fly to ride
much higher in the water than the fly line, defeating the purpose of the sinking line.
I normally use a three-foot piece of twelve-pound test looped into a short (one-foot)
permanent butt section at the end of the sinking line, making the entire leader a little
less than four feet in length.

BIG-GAME LEADERS

A standard saltwater leader is no more than a beefed-up version of a freshwater
tapered leader, and it's called "standard" because it is the leader configuration used
for most fish conditions. However, when fishing for large fish that will test the limits of your tackle—fish such as cobia, amberjack, and tarpon—you will want to use
what has become known as a big-game leader. A big-game leader is constructed so
that you can utilize every bit of the strength of the test tippet used in the leader. It's
constructed so that there is a "shock tippet" of either heavy monofilament or wire
between the test tippet and the fly.

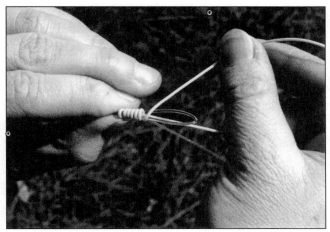

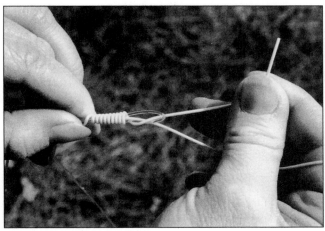

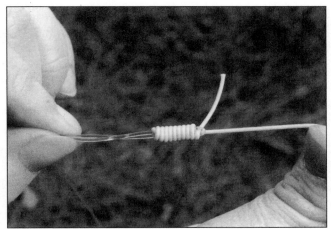

ALBRIGHT KNOT The Albright Knot can also be used to attach heavy monofilament to a doubled test tippet. The Albright is especially useful, however, since it can also be used to attach coated steel and single-strand steel wire to the test tippet. This is a very important and simple knot.

You can buy pretied big-game leaders, but shame on you if you do. They are, with a little practice, easy to tie, and if you should lose a fish because of leader failure, you will have only yourself to blame. Big-game leaders are constructed by tying a Bimini Twist at each end of a section of test tippet (eight-, twelve-, sixteen-pound test, and so on). I like my length of test tippet between the Bimini Twists to be between two and three feet long, and I like the loops formed by the Bimini Twist to be approximately twelve inches in length (see page 69). The loop end of one Bimini Twist is doubled back against itself, and a Surgeon's Loop is tied, giving you two strands of the test tippet instead of one. The other Bimini Twist loop is joined to your shock tippet. Your shock tippet will be made either of heavy monofilament or of wire. For tarpon, amberjack, cobia, and large red drum—all hard-fighting fish with rough mouths—you will want to choose a shock tippet of heavy monofilament testing from fifty to one hundred pounds. The knot of choice for joining your second Bimini Twist loop to your shock tippet is the Huffnagle. This knot was perfected by legendary Keys guide Steve Huff (see diagram). A good alternative is the Albright

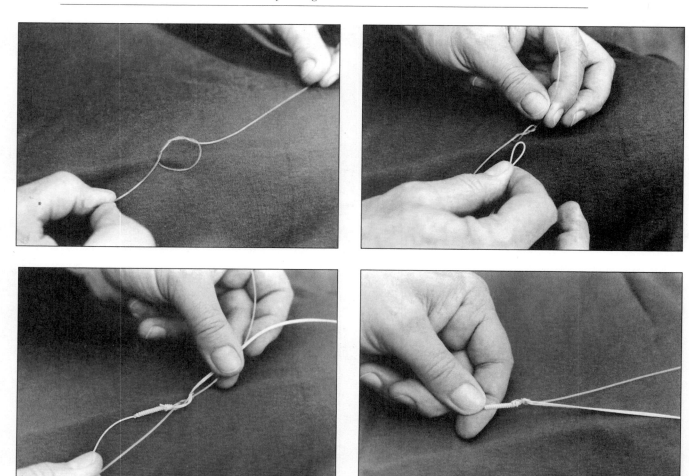

HUFFNAGLE KNOT The Huffnagle as shown in the diagram is used to connect a heavy shock tippet (fifty-plus pounds) to a double line. The double line is usually formed by putting a Bimini Twist at the end of the test tippet. The Huffnagle and the Albright Knot are both excellent knots, but the Huffnagle has a slightly smaller profile, making it the author's preference.

Special (see diagram). Heavy monofilament shock tippets (50 pound test and heavier) are tied to the fly with a three-and-a-half-turn Clinch Knot (see page 79).

If you are going to be seeking large, toothy fish such as sharks, large bluefish, barracuda, or king mackerel, you will want to use a piece of solid wire or coated wire testing thirty to sixty pounds. Both the coated wire and the solid wire are joined to the Bimini Twist with the Albright Special (see diagram). With coated multistrand wire, flies should be attached with a Figure Eight knot (see page 79). With solid wire, attach the fly with a Haywire Twist (see page 80).

If you are seeking record fish, there are several things you will want to keep in mind when constructing either a standard saltwater leader or a big-game leader. The tippet classes of the IGFA for fly fishing are figured in kilograms, but in pounds they approximate the following: two-, four-, six-, eight-, twelve-, sixteen-, and twenty-pound test. To be eligible for an IGFA record, the leader must contain at least fifteen inches of the test tippet. If you use a shock tippet of either wire or heavy monofila-

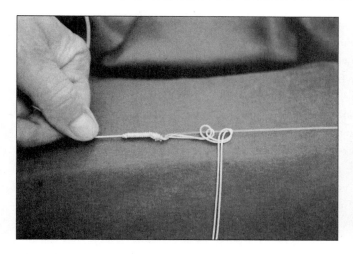
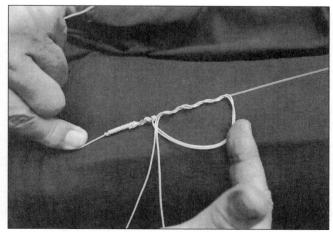

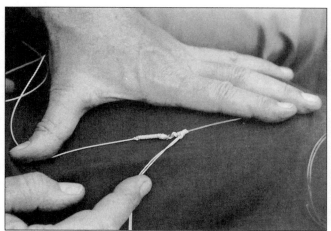
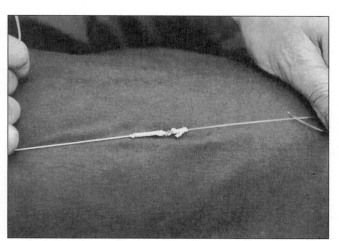

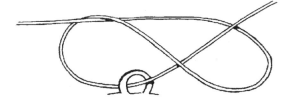

THREE-AND-A-HALF-TURN CLINCH KNOT *This version of the Clinch Knot is used to tie heavy monofilament (50-pound test and greater) directly to the fly. Heavy monofilament are used as shock tippets in big-game leaders.*

FIGURE EIGHT KNOT *This knot is used to attach plastic-coated steel leaders to the fly. As shown in the diagram, it is very simple and very effective. Plastic-coated leaders can be used for big bluefish, king mackerel, and other toothy critters.*

ment, there must be no more than twelve inches from the eye of the hook to the single-strand test tippet. It is no more difficult to tie a leader that meets IGFA standards than it is to tie one that doesn't. However, fly fishing is supposed to be fun. Don't get "hung up" trying to tie perfectly proportioned leaders in a heaving boat. Tie the best leader you can and keep fishing.

Much of your success and enjoyment on a fishing trip can depend on how well you prepared before departing. Making sure that your fly lines are ready to go—with a Bobbin Whip Loop at one end, and a short monofilament butt section with a loop at the other end—will save lots of time. Pre-tied leaders in marked plastic bags will also help to lower blood-pressure levels. It is far more pleasant to prepare lines and leaders in the comfort of one's own home than during a bluefish blitz, where time speeds up and finger skills become nonexistent.

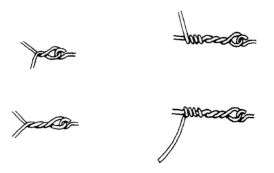

HAYWIRE TWIST This simple knot shown in the diagram is not really a knot, but a method of twisting solid steel wire when steel is needed as a shock tippet. Solid steel wire is needed for large barracuda and sharks.

CHAPTER 10

MUST- AND OUGHT'A-HAVE ACCESSORIES

Fishermen have always been gadget lovers. Largemouth bass fishermen, trout fishermen, surf fishermen, and live baiters have all been easy marks for the gadget industry. Saltwater fly fishermen are no different. With every new catalog there seem to be at least two or three extra pages of items that no self-respecting fly rodder should be without.

Hurrah for gadgets! I freely admit to having been first in line for many "must-have" items. The fly fisher can get tide-predicting watches, leader straighteners, fish-weight calculators, and a huge array of color-coordinated, monogrammed, sun-

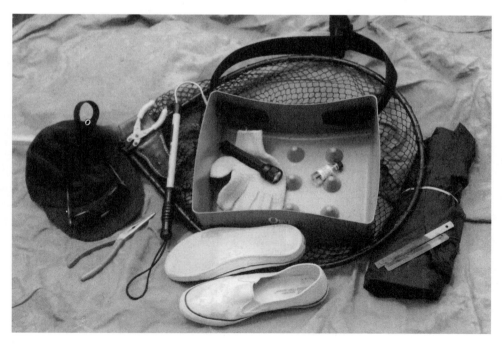

The must- and ought'a-have items shown in this photograph need not be expensive, but each can make your day safer and more pleasant.
Photograph by Tom Earnhardt

The angler in the foreground appears to be doing everything right except for one thing: Always wear sunglasses or eye protection when using a fly rod.
Photograph by Tom Earnhardt

blocking, hundred-dollar fishing shirts. For an angler just beginning to use a fly rod in salt water, whether in New Jersey or Texas, there are in fact, a few things that you shouldn't be without, and a few more things that you "ought'a have." Since I have been a conspicuous consumer of gadgets over the years, I have had to think long and hard about those things that are true necessities and about those things that I use on a regular basis. In the paragraphs that follow, I am not going to be patronizing and talk about all the nice things that people carry to make a day on the water more fun. There will be no discussions of sunscreen, first-aid kits, or small autofocus cameras to record your catch. I am going to stick just to the items that, in my opinion, are critical to your success and safety as a saltwater fly fisherman. It goes without saying that the following discussion is about "accessories" and not about the basics I've already mentioned—a decent fly rod, reel, line, and a selection of flies.

MUST-HAVE ACCESSORIES

If you are already a fisherman, you probably have some of my must-have items. The first, and I believe the most important, piece of equipment that a saltwater fly rodder can own is a good pair of polarized sunglasses. No dissertation is needed about the attributes of polarized glasses, which allow any angler to see fish better in the water. You can pay a lot of money for designer sunglasses that promise 100 percent UV protection, but if they aren't polarized, you're wasting your dollars.

For most conditions I prefer polarized glasses with brown or amber lenses. However, if you are going to be fishing over very light, bright bottoms, you will find the gray lenses more soothing to your eyes. You will also quickly find, if you haven't bought polarized glasses before, that you can pay less than twenty dollars or much more than a hundred dollars for a nonprescription pair. Although there is often a difference in quality based on the price, any pair of polarized glasses is better than none at all.

Polarized glasses are important for seeing fish, but of even greater importance is eye protection. Saltwater fly rodders typically use large flies in windy conditions. No matter how good your casting skills, there is a chance for tragedy as a fly line and fly pass back and forth beside your head. If you plan to fish during low light periods, or at night, when dark glasses are of little use, there is a solution. Clear plastic "shop" glasses, or yellow plastic shooting glasses should be worn to protect your eyes.

The next item on my must-have list is another simple one that most anglers already have—a good hat with a bill or brim. Whether you use a "flats" style hat with a long bill and a turn-down flap in the back, a baseball hat, or a broad-brimmed sun hat, the benefits are the same. Like glasses, a hat provides more protection for your head and face and helps you see better on flats, in the surf, or in the Gulf Stream. Make sure that you choose a hat with a brim or bill that has a dark underside—gray, black, or green. Light colors, such as white or tan, reflect and distort your view of the water.

The third most important piece of equipment a saltwater fly fisherman can carry is a good pair of small pliers that grip, mash, and cut. I have a pair of pliers in a holster that has accompanied me for almost a decade now. They are rusted in places and don't have the cutting edge they used to, but because I give them a few periodic squirts of WD-40, they are more than adequate for my needs. A decent pair of pliers can do a lot of things for you. On any given day you will use the cutter to trim your leaders and knots. The jaws will be used to mash down barbs and to remove hooks from the jaws of fish, or from your own hide. In recent years fishing pliers that cost a small fortune have appeared on the market. They have ball bearings and blades that are guaranteed to cut wire into the twenty-first century. My inexpensive pliers in their inexpensive holster have been more than adequate for lots of tarpon, cobia, drum, and striper fishing . . . but down deep, I really would like to have a pair of those "super pliers" someday.

The fourth item that I never leave home without is a small hook file. Whether I am standing in the surf or fishing from a boat, I use a file almost every time I change or check flies. When I put on a new fly, one of several small, fine-cutting mill files that I own appears instantly in my right hand. Whether you are fishing for hard-mouthed fish, such as tarpon; toothy fish, such as blues; or soft-mouthed weakfish, you should always make sure your hook is sharp (see chapter 6 for sharpening technique). The test of a sharp hook is whether it "bites" when pulled gently across your thumbnail. Sharp hooks will mean a lot more hookups. Even if you carry flies with presharpened hooks, oysters, rocks, and goblins will dull points, making a file necessary.

The final must-have item on my list is a good rain suit. Rain gear, either in the poncho style or a two-piece rain suit, will save your day and your trip. Whether you are fishing on a raw day on the Jersey shore or on a balmy day up a Georgia tidal creek, carry your rain gear. A good rain suit—and I prefer the two-piece styles—will not only keep you dry but will also serve as a wind-cutting shell on boat trips or during a thunderstorm. It is easy to get chilled, and there is no better protection than a rain suit. Mine is always stowed tightly rolled in the bottom of a small backpack that accompanies me everywhere I fish.

There are certainly many more items I carry on every fishing trip, but along with my tackle, none is as important as these five items. All of them are used by the fly fisher whether on a boat, jetty, or flat. Don't leave home without them.

OUGHT'A-HAVE ITEMS

The "ought'a-have" items that follow, though not absolute necessities, are, in my opinion, among the most important accessories to protect fish and anglers, or to make fly fishing more enjoyable. You will note that my ought'a-have items do not include a great pair of waders, a nice boat, or a copy of this book.

My first ought'a-have is a shooting basket. Whether you wade or fish from a boat, some kind of shooting basket will help control your line when wind and water are determined to tangle it. Early in this book I told a story about being marooned on a small island in Pamlico Sound in the late sixties. Even then I was aware of the need for a shooting basket, which was no more than a rectangular plastic wash pan attached to my waist with an army belt. When casting and retrieving, a shooting basket should be turned so that it is directly in front of your waist, or on the side of your stripping hand. Retrieved line falls in the basket rather than at your feet, in the surf, in marsh grass, or on the deck of a cluttered boat. When fighting fish, anglers often turn a shooting basket to their rear. Some find it more comfortable to take off a basket if they are into a long-fighting fish.

Shooting baskets have changed very little since I first began using them, except for the fact that enterprising anglers continue to improve them by putting indoor-outdoor carpeting in the bottom, or by sticking short pieces of heavy monofilament through the bottom of the basket. The carpet or monofilament keeps line from sliding around and wadding up in the basket. One well-known company even advertises a shooting basket designed at MIT with small cones in the bottom. Other manufacturers have soft, pliable mesh baskets that stow away in a small pouch. Today, all good baskets, whether homemade or expensive, have one thing in common—a quick-release buckle. A quick-release belt is necessary if you happen to fall into the water or step into a marsh hole. I have yet to meet anyone who can swim well wearing a shooting basket.

The next category of ought'a-have equipment is proper footwear. There are so many types of saltwater fly fishing, it is simply impossible to cover in a short space all of the types of footwear available to anglers. Suffice it to say that, just as in trout fishing, where you can bust your butt on slick rocks and boulders, saltwater fly rodding also offers you plenty of opportunities to hurt yourself. For example, if you are going

INSHORE AND NEARSHORE SPECIES

GREATER AMBERJACK
(Seriola dumerili)

These large schooling fish, often reaching more than 100 pounds, tend to concentrate around reefs, wrecks, and live bottom. Although they usually prefer water deeper than 60 feet, they will often move into shallow waters off inlets and beaches to forage on schools of menhaden and other inshore school fish. They are very curious and will sometimes swim near a boat and can usually be excited into taking a large streamer pattern or popper. Heavy monofilament shock tippets are necessary.

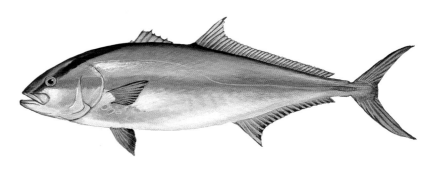

TARPON
(Megalops atlanticus)
a.k.a. Silver King

Along with bonefish, this is the premier fish of the Florida Keys and the west coast of Florida, but tarpon are also found in inshore waters during the summer from Virginia's eastern shore to Florida and all along the Gulf Coast. Relatively few tarpon have been caught on flies north of Florida, but anglers fishing in the shallow waters behind the barrier islands from Virginia south and all along the Gulf Coast are beginning to target tarpon in an attempt to develop new predictable fisheries for fly rodders.

JACK CREVALLE
(Caranx hippos)
a.k.a. Jack

Jacks are terrific fly-rod fish found in warm waters from the Chesapeake to Florida and all along the Gulf Coast. They are especially fond of surface poppers. Jacks are sometimes seen in inlets and off beaches simply finning and acting very lethargic. Other times they actively feed on any school of hapless baitfish. They often come into sounds, inlets, and harbors. Charleston Harbor has a large summer population of jacks weighing up to 35 pounds, so why go to Christmas Island for trevally, which is a close cousin?

FALSE ALBACORE
(Euthynnus alletteratus)
a.k.a. Little Tunny, Spotted Bonito, "Fat Albert"

These fantastic fish migrate north through mid-Atlantic coastal waters in the spring and south through the fall. At sea they can make up huge schools of up to a mile across. Inshore they break up into small pods that eat squid, crustaceans, mullet, and silversides. "Alberts" provide the greatest excitement when caught in the surf and around inlets in shallow water. In the Northeast a ten-pound little tunny is a good one; however, along the North Carolina coast, they will often average in the mid-teens during the late fall. In shallow water these fish will take 200 yards of backing and are much faster than bonefish. This is one of the author's favorite inshore species.

ATLANTIC BONITO
(Sarda sarda)
a.k.a. Bonito

They are often found in the same waters and under the same conditions as false albacore. They are great fly-rod fish at roughly two thirds the weight of their larger cousins. Like false albacore, they are voracious feeders and will keep eating when it appears there is no more room for anything in their stomachs. Surf Candies and small Clouser Minnows are ideal flies for bonito and false albacore. They are leader shy so flies should be tied directly to 10- or 12-pound monofilament.

NEARSHORE AND OFFSHORE SPECIES

GREAT BARRACUDA
(Sphyraena barracuda)
a.k.a Cuda

The great barracuda is found from the middle Atlantic region south and all along the Gulf Coast during warmer seasons. They love high-profile bottom, wrecks, and water temperatures approaching seventy degrees. Barracuda are extraordinarily fast and have perhaps the best cutting teeth in the ocean. The cuda has long been a favorite of flats fishermen in the Florida Keys and the Bahamas. It is becoming increasingly favored by fly fishermen on the East and Gulf coasts because of its lightening strikes and great jumps.

YELLOWFIN TUNA
(Thunnus albacares)
a.k.a. Allison Tuna, Longfin Tuna

Yellowfin are fantastic bluewater (deepwater) fish found from Massachusetts south, all along the Gulf Coast and in the Pacific. They have become a target for fly fishermen on "long-range boats" leaving Southern California. They are also thick enough at times off the Atlantic and Gulf coasts for fly rodders to have a legitimate shot at them. A yellowfin tuna in the 50- or 60-pound class is a test for any fly tackle.

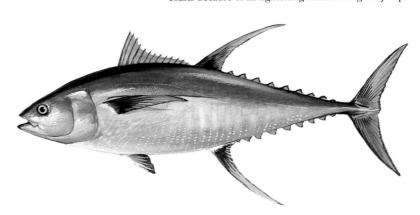

DOLPHIN
(Coryphaena hippurus)
a.k.a. Common Dolphin, Mahi Mahi, Dorado

From New Jersey south and all along the Gulf Coast, dolphin from 2 to 50 pounds can be found under sargassum and any other floating matter near blue water. These schooling fish will eat almost anything, from flying fish to crabs. This is the most predictable offshore fish for fly rodders.

SAILFISH
(Istiophorus platypterus)
a.k.a. Sail

Compared with marlins, sailfish are more of a nearshore species usually found in water ranging from 100 to 300 feet. Although they are more often caught by fly rodders off Central America, where their numbers are greater, they are still frequent targets of fly fishermen along the East and Gulf coasts. Atlantic sailfish average less than 50 pounds but put on spectacular aerial shows. Trolled hookless teasers are usually necessary to bring them within casting range.

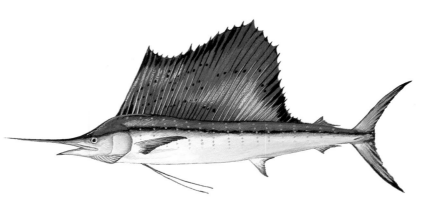

WHITE MARLIN
(Tetrapturus albidus)

White marlin are caught all along the East Coast and the Gulf of Mexico. There are major fishing areas out of Ocean City, Maryland, off the Outer Banks of North Carolina, and in Florida. Although these fish do not "turn on" as well as sailfish, they are still considered a fly-rod target and a real prize for any offshore fly angler.

INSHORE SPECIES

STRIPED BASS
(Morone saxatilis)
a.k.a. Striper, Rockfish, Rock

The striper is an anadromous fish that has also been introduced and done well in rivers and lakes throughout the world. It is one of the premier fish for fly rodders and can be caught along rocky shore lines, in the surf, near bridge pilings, and even far up coastal rivers. Menhaden, herring, silversides, and squid are preferred foods. Big fish are frequently caught at night. The Northeast (New Jersey to Maine), the Chesapeake Bay, and the San Francisco Bay offer some of the best options for fly rodders. Because of conservation efforts stocks are now on the rebound after years of decline.

SPOTTED SEA TROUT
(Cynoscion nedulosus)
a.k.a. Speckled Trout, Specs, Southern Weakfish

Related to drums, they can tolerate a wide range of salinity and can be caught from the surf to brackish estuaries. Specs are found on both the East and Gulf coasts. It is a prized fly-rod fish from the Chesapeake Bay to Florida and along the Gulf Coast. Called a "weakfish" because of its very tender mouth, these fish love grass, pilings, and shell banks. Finger mullet, menhaden, crabs, and shrimp are on their menu.

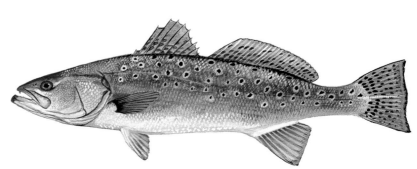

WEAKFISH
(Cynoscion regalis)
a.k.a. Gray Trout, Squeteague

These fish are found from Mobile, Alabama to Cape Cod, but are more abundant from South Carolina northward. Grays tend to prefer mud bottoms and deeper waters in the southern part of their range, but can also be a "flats fish" in the Northeast.

RED DRUM
(Sciaenops ocellatus)
a.k.a. Spottail Bass, Redfish, Channel Bass, Reds

An outstanding fly-rod fish, the red is found all along the Atlanticand Gulf coasts. It is distinctive because of its inferior mouth (down turned) and large spots on the tail or body, and is called "redfish" because of the coppery color exhibited by most adults. Redfish are quickly becoming the "flats fish" of the south Atlantic and Gulf Coast states because of their preference for shallow water, grass beds, and oyster bars. Crab, shrimp, and mullet imitations are always productive.

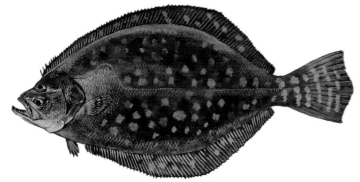

SOUTHERN FLOUNDER
(Paralichthys lethostigma)
a.k.a. Flounder and Flatfish

This species is closely related to the summer flounder and Gulf flounder. All of the flounders spend time in shallow inshore water and some often move into slightly brackish water. Flounders are not usually a target fish for fly rodders but are a secondary catch for anglers seeking red drum and weak-fish. Nothing beats a Clouser Minnow hopped on the bottom for flounder.

INSHORE AND NEARSHORE SPECIES

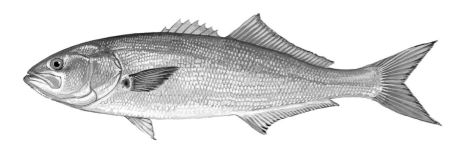

BLUEFISH
(Pomatomas saltatrix)
a.k.a. Blue, Snapper, Chopper

Found in many parts of the world, in the United States blues are largely confined to the East Coast from Maine to Florida. They are voracious feeders that usually feed in packs. Larger fish tend to congregate in the northern part of the range from the Carolinas north. This is one fish for which fly rodders must use wire tippets, especially when pursuing larger bluefish (up to 20 pounds). Small blues are a great "starter" fish for new fly rodders because of their aggressiveness. Save your expensive flies for more finicky fish.

COBIA
(Rachycentron canadum)
a.k.a. Lemonfish, Ling, Cabio

This fish is becoming a favorite of inshore fly rodders from Virginia south and all along the Gulf Coast. Because they can range up to 100 pounds, this is truly an inshore big game-fish. Cobia are caught over wrecks, under buoys, and near jetties. They tag along with large turtles and rays, and are often seen on the surface as "free swimmers" in inlets and bays. Cobia are very strong fish and one of the author's favorite inshore fly-rod targets.

KING MACKEREL
(Scomberomorus cavalla)
a.k.a. Kingfish, King

This is the largest of Atlantic mackerel, preferring the waters from Virginia south and along the Gulf Coast. They love warm water and are attracted to inlets and nearshore wrecks by schools of menhaden, mullet, and other surface-schooling fish. This is one of the most exciting fish available to saltwater fly rodders, but they must usually be coaxed into casting distance by chumming. The razor-sharp teeth of all king mackerel make wire tippets a necessity. Any fish over 30 pounds is a large one, but kings can range up to 100 pounds.

SPANISH MACKEREL
(Scomberomorus maculatus)
a.k.a. Spanish

Spanish prefer warm water and are found from New York south on the East Coast and all along the Gulf Coast. They are much smaller than their kingfish cousins and seldom exceed five pounds. They are usually found forcing anchovies, mullet, and other schooling fish to the surface. Although they have sharp teeth and can cut through monofilament leaders, most fly rodders tie flies directly to monofilament because Spanish are extremely "leader shy."

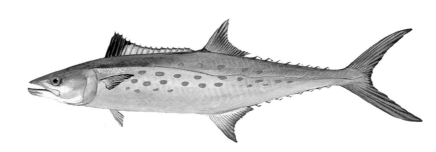

LADYFISH
(Elops saurus)

These slender fish, often reaching up to 30 inches in length, remind fly rodders of miniature tarpon. They are found during warm weather along the East and Gulf coasts in inlets and often far up into tidal creeks. They are especially aggressive when popping bugs are used. Charleston Harbor, from June through August, has one of the best ladyfish concentrations. Farther south, the Indian River Estuary is another hot spot for these jumpers.

Del Brown's Merkin

M.O.E. Fly
(Mother of Epoxy)

Ultra Shrimp

Pompano Puff

Krystal Minnow

Alba Clouser

Mihulka Sand Eel

McCrab

Super Squid

Banded Shrimp

Glass Minnow

Rubber Candy

Surf Candy

Bonito Bait

CRUSTACEANS, SQUID, EELS, and SLENDER-PROFILE BAITFISH (Anchovies, Sardines, etc.)

DEL BROWN'S MERKIN
(Tied by the author)—A crab fly originally tied for permit by master angler Del Brown, it is now the ticket to any fish that likes crabs. Tie it in colors from tan, to yellow, to olive in sizes 4 to 3/0. The author has taken redfish, sea trout, sheepshead, dolphin, and stripers on this pattern. It is a redfish favorite on the flats of South Carolina and Georgia. It is on the author's top-ten list of most useful saltwater patterns.

McCRAB
Here is another permit fly, designed by Montana angler George Anderson, that has also found its way to waters with no permit. This pattern, made of clipped deer hair, was one of the first great crab imitations, and will take any crab eater.

M.O.E. FLY (Mother of Epoxy)
This is a bonefish/permit fly developed in Florida that is now used far away from the Keys. The M.O.E. is tied in a variety of sizes and colors and will take fish that eat crustaceans.

SUPER SQUID
(Tied by the author)—The squid fly tied in white or tan, in sizes 2 to 2/0, is the author's best dolphin fly. It can also be an excellent fly for false albacore and stripers. It is a variation of some of the great squid flies developed in New England.

ULTRA SHRIMP
Here is another epoxy pattern from Bob Popovics. In its many variations, it will take any shrimp eater from bonefish to sea trout.

POMPANO PUFF
(Tied by the author)—Tied with orange or yellow marabou on weighted size 6 and 8 hooks, it is a deadly fly for pompano in the surf. These variations of traditional bonefish flies are used by the author for pompano on rods matched to a 5- or 6-weight line.

BANDED SHRIMP
This is a terrific shrimp pattern the author found in a Texas fly shop several years ago. It's an excellent pattern for redfish and sea trout. Dolphin love it, too.

KRYSTAL MINNOW
Try this gaudy but simple pattern in various colors for stripers, blues, and albacore. The wing is all Krystal Flash.

GLASS MINNOW
(Tied by Brian Horsley)—This is a proven pattern for false albacore, Atlantic bonito, blues, Spanish mackerel, and stripers. This is a variation of a similar fly designed by Chico Fernandez.

ALBA CLOUSER
(Tied by the author)—In the author's experience, this is simply the best false albacore fly there is! Note that it is tied with silver-and-black painted eyes on hook sizes 4, 2, and 1/0. The best colors are green/silver/clear and chartreuse/gold/clear Ultrahair. It is also a terrific fly for Spanish mackerel, school stripers, and anything else that likes "silversides."

RUBBER CANDY
(Tied by Bob Popovics)—Here is another extraordinarily innovative pattern from master tier Bob Popovics. Tied in a variety of sizes and colors, this pattern is good for albacore, weakfish, stripers, mackerel, blues, etc. The head is made of clear silicone, not epoxy.

MIHULKA SAND EEL
Now that the stripers are back, eel patterns have proven to be a favorite in the Northeast, the lower Chesapeake Bay, and along the North Carolina Outer Banks. Although designed for stripers in size 3/0, they are also very effective on big bluefish.

SURF CANDY
(Tied by Bob Popovics)—An early Popovics creation that rates a spot on the author's top ten of saltwater flies. When tied in various profiles, it can be an anchovy or a sand eel. The one shown is a "rain minnow" imitation Popovics tied for bonito and false albacore. It is also a durable fly for Spanish mackerel.

BONITO BAIT
Sometimes big fish want tiny baits. This pattern tied on a size-6 hook is great for bonito and false albacore when they are feeding on immature glass minnows.

Chugger

Striper Special

Popovics Bangers

Dink

Diver-Swimmer

Offshore Sliding
Popper Head

Classic Popper

Pencil Popper

Slider

Alba Streaker

Braided
Needlefish

TOPSIDE IN THE SALT (Poppers, Sliders, and Streakers)

CHUGGER
(Tied by Lucky Day Lures)—Large-faced poppers, often referred to as chuggers, move lots of water and make lots of noise, exciting large fish. Large faces are especially good for amberjack, cobia, and other wreck dwellers. They are tied in an infinite variety of colors and always in large sizes, 3/0 to 6/0.

OFFSHORE SLIDING POPPER HEAD
Large styrofoam sliding heads are used on leaders ahead of streamers such as big Deceivers. Although they were developed for billfish, they are also useful for other fish that want a mouthful, such as amberjack, cobia, and large bluefish.

STRIPER SPECIAL
(Tied by the author)—This fly, a skipping bug, is one of the author's favorites for striped bass and large bluefish. It is tied in a variety of colors; but white, blue, and black seem to be the most effective. The slender profile and the sparse tail make it an easy bug to cast. This fly is tied in sizes 1/0 and 3/0.

CLASSIC POPPER
(Body by Edgewater)—This soft foam body with a hollowed-out face makes lots of noise. It is a favorite in the Northeast for stripers and blues. In black it is a great dirty-water fly and night fly. In chartreuse and white there is no better all-purpose saltwater popper.

POPOVICS BANGERS
This series of poppers in a variety of colors comes from the vise of Bob Popovics. Bangers are good for any fish that like noise and flash. They should be illegal for blues and jack cravelle.

PENCIL POPPER
(Body by Edgewater)—Pencil poppers have long been favorites of surf fly rodders. They cast extremely well because of their slim profile, yet seem to create the right noise for many gamefish. Another striper favorite.

DINK
(Body by Edgewater)—Even little poppers have a place in saltwater. The dink is excellent for both speckled sea trout and redfish in calm water. It can also be used with a small "trailer" fly tied to it.

SLIDER
(Body by Edgewater)—Sliders have proved to be very effective in calm, shallow water for redfish and speckled trout. They "slide" through the water with little noise rather than causing a "chugging" sound.

DIVER-SWIMMER
(Tied by Buzz Bryson)—This soft foam fly with its protruding forward lip digs in and swims during a steady retrieve, but floats to the surface when the retrieve is stopped. Great for stripers in white and chartreuse. The brown and gold shown on the colorplate is a good color for redfish.

ALBA STREAKER
(Tied by the author)—This fly tied in size 1 using small diameter PVC tubing is a terrific fly for false albacore, bonito, and Spanish mackerel. It should be retrieved rapidly. The author developed this fly for use in rough waters near inlets and shoals on North Carolina's Outer Banks.

BRAIDED NEEDLEFISH
Braided flies of up to a foot in length, in sizes 1/0 or 2/0 in chartreuse or orange, have long been among the most effective barracuda flies. Similar long flies without the braid are also effective. These flies are usually thrown 10 to 15 feet away from barracuda and retrieved very fast. A fly cannot be retrieved too fast for barracuda.

LARGE-PROFILE FLIES (MENHADEN, MULLET, PINFISH, ETC.)

Whistler

Poplips

3-D

Siliclone

Woolhead Mullet

Lefty's Deceiver

Abel's Anchory

Key's Tarpon Fly

Blanton's Sar-Mul-Mak

WHISTLER
(Tied by the author)—This pattern tied in varied color combinations in sizes 1/0 to 5/0 was created by Dan Blanton for San Francisco Bay stripers. After becoming a mainstay of Central American tarpon fishermen, it has now found its way to the East Coast and the Gulf Coast, where it is a great fly for cobia, red drum, amberjack, and sea trout. The whistler "pushes" water, making it an excellent choice for dirty water and deep water.

LEFTY'S DECEIVER
(Tied by Brian Horsley)—This is Lefty Kreh's universal pattern, which is used for almost anything that swims. The deceiver is not a pattern but a method of tying that keeps the fly from fouling. It is tied in every color combination imaginable and can be tied in lengths ranging from one inch to one foot. This should be the first saltwater pattern in your box.

POPLIPS
(Tied by Bob Popovics)—Popovics' terrific bunker imitation is great for stripers, blues, king mackerel, and anything else that eats menhaden. Good in any color, it is especially effective in chartreuse and purple/white in sizes 2/0 to 5/0.

ABEL'S ANCHOVY
First tied by Steve Abel (Abel Reels), it is now a universal fly for tarpon, bluefish, dolphin, stripers, and sharks. The pattern can be tied in sizes 2 to 5/0.

3-D
(Tied by Bob Popovics)—This is another excellent bunker (menhaden) imitation good for blues, king mackerel, stripers, cobia, and many other large fish. It can be tied in sizes 2/0 to 5/0, and a trailer hook can be used.

SILICLONE
(Tied by Bob Popovics)—The round profile of this fly makes it a seductive mullet imitation in many colors and sizes (1/0 to 5/0). It is a real producer fly for blues, stripers, jacks, and anything else that eats mullet.

KEY'S TARPON FLY
(Tied by the author)—The "tarpon fly" is also a method of tying rather than a specific fly. Key's tarpon flies in sizes 1/0 to 5/0 were first designed for the flats. Tarpon flies are now used on all coasts for such fish as dolphin, red drum, cobia, bluefish, and stripers. These flies, tied in all colors, have a great pulsating action and are close to foul-proof.

WOOLHEAD MULLET
(Tied by the author)—A similar fly can be tied with a deer hair head in sizes 1 to 4/0. These generic mullet patterns in gray and white are good fished inshore and offshore. It is a good fly for large sea trout, stripers, and bluefish.

BLANTON'S SAR-MUL-MAK
West Coast guru Dan Blanton created this universal pattern. When tied in various colors and dressings, either sparse or full, they can represent a sardine, mullet, or mackerel. Don't leave home without them.

Mike's Red Gold — MirrOlure Fly

Diving Shiner — Dahlberg

Squirm Fly — Sea Ducer

Slick Water Fly

Hot Flash Bend Back — Rattle Rouser

Wobble Fly

Marabou Bend Back

Clouser Deep Minnow

Danny's Redfish Special

SKINNY WATER FLIES

MIKE'S RED GOLD
(Tied by the author)—This is a simple but effective redfish fly designed by Captain Mike Able for South Carolina and Georgia flats fishing. The weighted shank dressed only with gold Flashabou causes the hook to ride up. It is tied in sizes 4 to 2/0 and is especially good in dirty water.

MIRROLURE FLY
(Tied by Brian Horsley)—This is a proven fly for surf or marsh in sizes 1 to 3/0. It is a good "imitation" of the famous MirrOlure, perhaps the best spotted weakfish lure ever invented. It can be tied to match any MirrOlure color combination. Use this to match the "plastic hatch."

DIVING SHINER
(Tied by the author)—A shallow running fly, the shiner is great for redfish and trout in sizes 2 to 3/0. It is too good to feed to bluefish! This is the saltwater version of the marabou muddler minnow. In all white it is a great striper fly and is similar to the "snake flies" used in the Northeast.

DAHLBERG DIVER
(Tied by the author)—Originally a freshwater creation by Larry Dahlberg, it is a diving, swimming, undulating saltwater fish catcher in sizes 1 to 4/0. The diver is a great all-purpose pattern where swimming and stopping the fly is necessary to attract fish. This is a great fly for redfish, sea trout, stripers, cobia, tarpon, dolphin, etc.

SQUIRM FLY
(Tied by Ted Cabali)—The squirm is an unusual "grub" fly tied for Louisiana redfish and sea trout. It is tied in many colors, but black is especially good in off-color waters.

SLICK WATER FLY
(Tied by the author)—This pattern tied with orange grizzly, red grizzly, and yellow grizzly is very effective in calm, clear water conditions when long leaders are needed. This fly works well from Texas to the Carolinas for reds and sea trout. It is a small pattern tied in sizes 2, 4, and 6.

SEADUCER
(Tied by the author)—This fly is a variation of the Homer Rhodes tarpon fly. Many variations of this pattern were developed by Chico Fernandez. It can be tied in sizes 2 to 4/0 and is effective for tarpon, sea trout, dolphin, etc. A simple, universal pattern.

HOT FLASH BEND BACK
(Tied by Brian Horsley)—Bend backs were first tied for bonefish and redfish in the Florida region. They are now used effectively all along the East Coast and Gulf Coast for any fish found in shallow waters. Variations of this pattern in a variety of colors and sizes are a must for any serious shallow-water fisherman.

WOBBLE FLY
(Tied by Bill Quenan)—This pattern, originated by Florida guide Jon Cave, is an "imitation" of the famous Johnson Gold Spoon. The gold spoon has long been a favorite of spin fishermen seeking redfish in grassy waters. The tantalizing wobble of this fly will take a variety of other species, too.

RATTLE ROUSER
(Tied by Kirk Dietrich)—This fly has a rattle capsule in its belly. They are the same rattles used in plastic worms for largemouth bass fishing. Dietrich created his rattling fly for redfish in Louisiana's tannin-stained waters. A noisy idea that will find its way into other flies.

CLOUSER DEEP MINNOW
(Tied by Brian Horsley)—The Clouser minnow in a variety of colors is simply the hottest fly fished both on flats and in deep waters in use today. The "Tomato Clouser" shown is especially effective for speckled trout in Virginia and the Carolinas. Other variations of the Clouser minnow in sizes 6 to 4/0 are used for almost every species that swims. The dumbbell eyes, which can be found in a variety of weights, cause the head to dip at the end of each strip during the retrieve.

DANNY'S REDFISH SPECIAL
(Tied by Captain Dennis Hammond)—One of the best flies in use for Indian River, Florida, redfish, this is another variation of the bend back that makes it virtually weedless even in thick grass. Various color combinations of this fly are also good for sea trout, bonefish, and even dolphin.

MARABOU BEND BACK
(Tied by the author)—Another variation of the bend back series of flies, it can be tied in a variety of colors—white/silver, chartreuse/gold, brown/gold, etc., in sizes 4 to 2/0. Because of the breathing action of marabou, the fly needs to be moved only slightly to attract redfish or other flats feeders. Dolphin and bluefish will also take this fly when it is drifted in a chum line.

Tarpon, among the most spectacular fish on any tackle, are available to anglers from Virginia's Eastern Shore south and along the Gulf Coast during summer months. *(Photographs by Tom Earnhardt.)*

Dan Blanton admires a San Francisco Bay striper caught at sunset. *(Photograph by Dan Blanton.)*

* Note on fly sizes: The Crayola crayons shown in each colorplate are exactly 3 5/8 inches long.

** Note on fly tiers: When known, the tier's name is given. Whenever possible, the "developer" of the pattern is named in the text.

*** Note on barbless hooks: For all fish the author mashes the barb on with pliers hooks. Barbless hooks actually penetrate better. From experience the author has found that flies stored in foam boxes travel better with barbs. Barbs are mashed at the time of use.

Just south of New Orleans the scenery is magnificent and the redfish willing in all but the coldest weather. Shallow draft "mud boats" are needed in the bayou country. *(Photograph by Captain Bubby Rodriguez.)*

Behind the barrier islands of South Carolina and Georgia is some of the country's best fly fishing for sea trout and redfish. *(Photograph by Captain Jerry Ciandella.)*

The Chesapeake Bay Light Tower is a gathering place for inshore and off-shore species . . . and fly fishermen. *(Photograph by Tom Earnhardt.)*

The Outer Banks is a land of lighthouses. Here Donnie Jones and daughter Rebecca work the waters near Cape Lookout Light. *(Photograph by Tom Earnhardt.)*

New Jersey jetties can provide thrills and spectacular fly fishing.
(Photograph by Ed Jaworowski.)

Lefty Kreh bears down on a false albacore on North Carolina's Outer Banks.
(Photograph by Tom Earnhardt.)

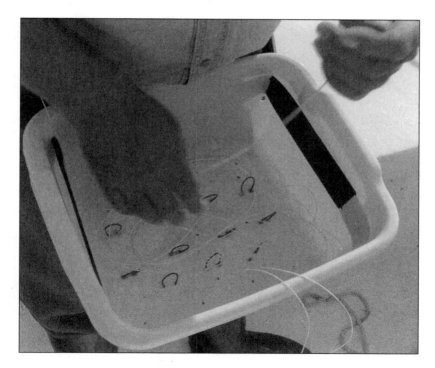

A very inexpensive shooting basket can be made from a plastic wash pan, loops of heavy "Weed Eater" monofilament, and a nylon utility belt. Along with his American Express Card, Bob Popovics never leaves home without his basket. Photographs by Tom Earnhardt

to fish on jetties or seawalls, make sure you have felt-bottomed shoes, at the very least—or even better, metal cleats to provide secure footing. A common sense thing!

There is no such thing as a nonskid boat deck. Whether you are on a center console in the Chesapeake Bay or on the bow of a Louisiana skiff, a good pair of deck shoes will greatly reduce your chance for serious injury. Deck shoes normally have relatively soft rubber bottoms and small, closely spaced treads, such as those found in Sperry Top-Siders. There are many serviceable shoes, sandals, and boots with the proper treads needed for safety. Tennis shoes, running shoes, gum-soled hunting shoes, and bare feet will fail you on a wet deck, especially when you add a layer of fish slime.

Other items on my ought'a-have list are safe-release devices for fish. When I say "safe," I am talking about safety for both fish and anglers. Before you can define what "safe" is in any given circumstance, you must know what the characteristics of your intended quarry are. Jack crevalle, redfish, and stripers all have surfaces inside the gill cover that can cut you badly. Other fish such as cobia and amberjack, although toothless, have very powerful crushers in their mouths that can mash a hand. Bluefish and barracuda have the teeth to ruin anyone's day. So how do you handle these fish when removing a fly?

There are several items that make unhooking and releasing much easier, especially when used with fishing pliers. A heavy coated glove, which you can stick into your pocket, is a good release tool for many fish such as speckled trout, redfish, amberjack, small cobia, stripers, and a variety of others. A firm grasp of the lower jaw immobilizes a number of fish. Even though the tail of a bonito or a false albacore can be grasped with one's bare hand without injury, grabbing these fish with a coated glove is more comfortable.

For some fish, such as large bluefish or barracuda, a small lip gaff slipped through the soft tissues behind the lower jaw will help protect the fish and the angler during release. In this category of safe-release items, probably the newest and most effective are the shallow, rubber-coated landing nets that allow many species of fish to be landed and released unhurt. Old-style knotted nylon nets tear the slime coat of almost any fish, and they can also cut into sensitive gill areas. The new small-mesh rubber-coated nets cradle a fish without cutting its slime coat. I have seen these nets used for weakfish, redfish, stripers, albacore, and, most recently, cobia. Claude Bain, director of the Virginia Sportfishing Tournament, began using large "muskie-size" coated small-mesh nets to release large cobia caught near the Bay Bridge Tunnel. Cobia have long been feared by many anglers because of their ability to trash equipment and tackle boxes with their strong tails. What Bain found out was that a large net, slipped under a cobia, allows the fish to be brought alongside or even in a boat with little struggle while it is unhooked. A wet towel placed over a fish's eyes will help it remain calm. The new shallow mesh nets are most definitely an "ought'a-have" item for any angler, especially those practicing catch-and-release.

Finally, every fly rodder should carry a small flashlight, whether or not you intend to fish at night. In the early morning, late afternoon, or during a heavy rain, extra light can help with knots, hook removal, motor repair, and other situations where a little light on the subject can make all the difference in the world.

As I mentioned earlier, these must-have and ought'a-have items for fly rodders are not intended to be an all-inclusive checklist. They are simply items that I am extremely uncomfortable being without. Needless to say, I carry many other items, including good fly boxes to protect my flies, cheap magnifying glasses for anglers over forty, leader-spool holders, a tape measure, a tube of Super Glue, and a small first-aid and medicine kit. To help carry many of these items, a fishing vest can be a useful addition to your wardrobe. As you read through this chapter, you probably decided that I left out something that, from your own experience, is equally necessary. I wrote this chapter not in an effort to be paternalistic, but in an effort to help you avoid some of the chills, puncture wounds, bruises, and fish cuts that I've inflicted on myself over the years.

PART IV

"SEEING", PRESENTATION, RETRIEVE, AND FIGHTING FAIR

CHAPTER 11

READING THE WATER
Understanding What You See

In the early 1970s I was Captain Nat Ragland's first paying customer (eighty-five dollars a day!). Captain Nat had long been an accomplished light-tackle and fly fisherman in the Miami area before moving to Marathon to team up with another guide. I still remember vividly my first day of tarpon fishing on Jack's Banks on the Gulf side of the Keys. Since this was in the days before poling towers, Nat and I were at approximately the same height above the water. Over and over again he would point, shout, and gesture: "Tarpon, one o'clock, eighty feet. They're moving left, and now they're at twelve o'clock at sixty feet. Cast. Cast."

The water was crystal clear and there was very little wind. To make matters even more embarrassing, Captain Nat was fifteen feet farther away from the fish than I was, since he was doing all of his sighting from the stern of the boat. I have twenty-twenty vision and I was wearing Polaroids, but I saw nothing and Nat seemed to see everything. On that first day I blew chance after chance by "lining" several schools and by casting to the tails of fish as they swam away. On the second day, with patient instruction from Nat, I began to understand that "seeing" did not always mean seeing fish in the water; "seeing" also included seeing shadows on the bottom, small "pushes" of water ahead of moving tarpon, and the wakes produced by schools or by individual fish.

On later trips with Nat and other guides, I learned that each fish in the Keys produces its own distinctive markers. There are muds, tails, and pushes of water by bonefish. Permit occasionally flash a sickle tail. I learned that around white holes there is often a stationary dark line—a barracuda.

Over the years the vast majority of my fly-fishing time has shifted to the Mid-Atlantic Coast, where the water is not so clear as in the Keys. There are, in fact, places where it is extremely difficult to see a fish in the water. The flats behind many South Carolina and Georgia barrier islands during the summer months are full of shrimp and mullet that keep the water muddied, making it almost impossible to see a red drum unless it runs aground. However, having fished with local experts, I finally learned to distinguish the wobbly wake and the push of a redfish in muddy water

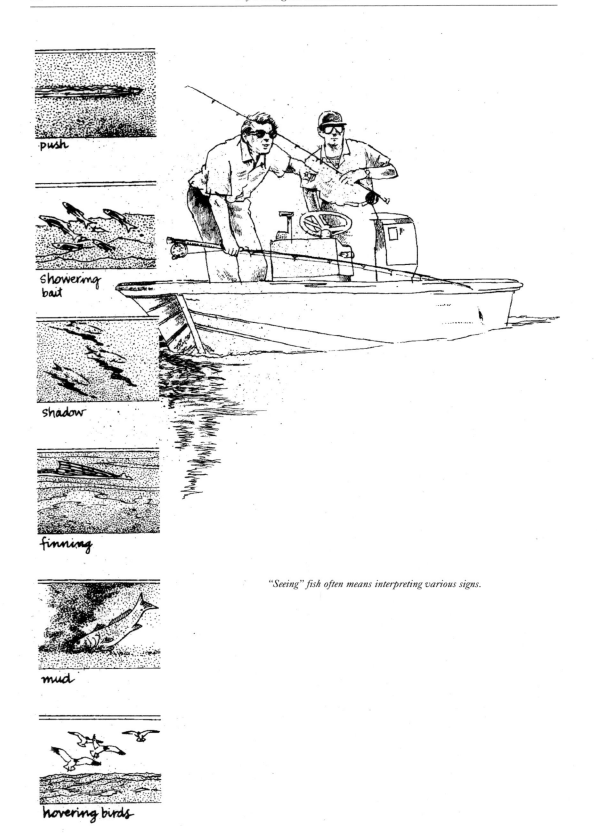

push

showering
bait

shadow

finning

mud

hovering birds

"Seeing" fish often means interpreting various signs.

from the "straight" wakes and pushes of a large mullet. In Louisiana the tannin-stained waters offer fabulous redfishing once you learn how to distinguish the movement of redfish from other critters occupying the same space.

When "Seeing" Doesn't Mean Seeing

With a number of years on the water behind me, I can now do a pretty good job identifying the different feeding patterns of bluefish, Spanish mackerel, and false albacore. The way baitfish are scattered, and the way birds hover over them offer clues. Feeding albacore may even provide sound effects in the form of a sharp "glug." The fact is that "seeing" fish is only partly a visual exercise. I think most guides and experienced fishermen would agree that what you see with your eyes, combined with your experiences, gives what amounts to an extra sense.

For example, in the lower Chesapeake Bay and in North Carolina inlets, during May and again in September, I like to search for slow-moving wakes near the surface on calm days. In the past, at a poor angle and distance, I could not tell for sure what fish were producing wakes, but my repeated experience in those locations at the same time of year now enables me to "see" moving cobia. Experience also tells me that showering finger mullet along a deep marsh bank at certain times of the year mean speckled trout. Captain Brian Horsley, a fly-fishing guide in the Nags Head region, will freely admit that when he says, "I see some specs working over there," he doesn't actually see speckled trout, but a number of signs that, when taken together, can mean nothing else but specs.

One of the exciting things about fly fishing is that, more than any other angling technique, it requires you either to visualize or to sense the location, movement, and direction of fish so that you can place your fly in the optimal position—for in fly fishing, fish must be given a look before they will eat. Don't forget, though, that it is much easier to learn to "see" with the help of others, whether they be guides or experienced anglers. As I indicated earlier, "seeing"—or developing that extra sense that fly fishermen must develop—does not often come quickly and easily. Once you learn the basics, however, you will become able to adapt quickly to the challenges of finding fish in almost any water. Whether you live near Tom's River, New Jersey, the eastern shore of Maryland and Virginia, or the great redfish/spec flats of Texas, the following "signs" should help you. Some of these signs are obvious and some are very subtle, but in the words of Lou Tabory, only "time on the water" will enable you to develop and expand your fish-sighting senses.

Birds. No matter where you fish in salt water, birds can be your best friends. Sometimes a flock of raucous gulls or pelicans will mark schools of bait being herded and attacked from below. Sometimes there are great numbers of birds; other times a single tern will betray the presence of a moving pod of bonito or false albacore. Offshore, a frigate bird may mark dolphin or a single billfish. Birds can also tell you when very little is happening on the surface. On countless trips I have passed productive fishing areas only to see hundreds of birds sitting or walking on the beach. On such occasions my dad would usually stop the boat, break out the food, and say, "People should eat when birds don't."

A feeding frenzy at the surface will wake up any fly fisherman.
Photograph by Tom Earnhardt

Showering Bait. Although not as visible at long distances as birds, showering bait is a great giveaway for the presence of feeding fish. Whether silversides, menhaden, mullet, or mud minnows, frightened baitfish are always a good sign for the fly rodder. It may be a few skittering baitfish or a major eruption in which baits explode in a noisy frenzy. Almost all fly-rod targets, from stripers to Spanish, will, depending on the season, be chasing a certain type of bait. Some feeding activity is very predictable with regard to season and tides. Other feeding activity is random. One August, my wife, young son, and I were behind our house on the North Carolina Outer Banks when, without warning, the water around our skiff simply exploded. Mullet went in every direction, and some even bounced off the side of the boat. The villains were jack crevalle in the fifteen- to twenty-five-pound range. I know because I was able to catch several on large Deceivers over the next hour and a half. Also, remember that not only do showering bait help you mark fish, the baitfish themselves give you an idea of the size and color of flies to use.

Tailing and Finning. When most fly rodders think of tailing fish, bonefish are the first that come to mind. Many other fish, however, show themselves by tailing and finning. From the Carolinas south and all along the Gulf Coast, no fish shows its tail more often than a redfish. In very shallow water they look as if they are standing on their heads. The tips of the tail or the dorsal fin of slow-moving cobia can be a give-away. Jack crevalle will sometimes appear to be basking and finning at the surface.

A number of fish will often give away their position by showing their dorsal or tail fin. Here a tarpon moves over a shallow bar. Photograph by Tom Earnhardt

Several years ago, during the spring, I remember standing in my boat near Cape Lookout looking at the exposed tails of large slow-moving bluefish just off the beach. Unusual, yes—but most fish will, at times, show themselves to observant anglers.

Nothing will make a fly fisherman take notice more quickly than the appearance of a tarpon as it rolls in shallow estuaries. Tarpon have to gulp air since roughly 30 percent of their oxygen is derived through rudimentary lungs. When a tarpon rolls, you first see his head, followed by his dorsal fin, and finally a small flip of his tail. As I mentioned earlier, there is as yet no truly predictable fly-rod fishery for tarpon outside of Florida, but large numbers of these fish appear in the estuaries along Virginia's eastern shore, behind North Carolina's Outer Banks, in the tidal creeks of South Carolina and Georgia, and in the Louisiana Delta. Because they show themselves in the summer months, and because they do eat flies, tarpon are on the "available" list for fly rodders outside of Florida.

Muds. One of the easiest ways of finding bonefish from a distance is to look for a white cloud of marl (mud) being kicked up by feeding fish. A number of fish, feeding on flats of the East and Gulf coasts, will also create muds. Many years ago I was spin fishing for spotted weakfish next to a drop-off in Pamlico Sound. On a nearby shoal I noticed a patch of muddy water over an acre in size. Without looking more closely, I assumed that the commotion was caused by a school of rays, which are notorious for kicking up muds. It was only after I saw a large tail appear in the mud that I realized

The dark spots under the surface that looks like part of an oil spill are tightly packed menhaden. Such schools of bait invariably mean that fly-rod targets are close at hand.
Photograph by Tom Earnhardt

it was a school of giant channel bass (redfish) rooting for crabs and shrimp. I quickly rigged a large Hopkins lure (metal squid) on a heavy spinning rig as the boat drifted within fifty feet of the mud. The first cast, and the only cast, produced a forty-pound channel bass. Oh, if I had only had a fly rod!

Pushes and Wakes. Among the most difficult signs for new fly rodders to read are pushes. Individual fish and schools of fish moving just under the surface will often displace water in a way that causes a small bulge or wave. Pushes caused by redfish, false albacore, bluefish, and stripers are sometimes easily discernible in slick water, but at other times they can best be described as "troubled waters." When there are wind-caused ripples or waves on the surface, skilled anglers can still pick out "trouble" caused by the motion of larger fish under the surface.

Closely related to, but different from, pushes are wakes. Wakes are the V-shaped trails left in the water as a fish swims under the surface. You don't need a well-trained eye in the Keys to tell the difference between the wake of a bonnet shark and that of a bonefish. On other coasts, though, anglers must learn the difference between the straight V-wake of a large mullet and the slower, wobbly line left by a redfish.

Color Changes. To the observant angler, schools of fish, both predators and baitfish, will produce color changes in the water. Some will be dramatic, like the dark-gray patches created by schools of tightly packed menhaden. Whenever you spot such a large gray mass, it is a good omen that a fly-rod fish cannot be far behind, even if there are no birds circling or baits leaving the water. A slow-moving brown line may indicate a school of cobia. A reddish or coppery mass several feet under the surface may be either rays or a school of red drum. Redfish guides look for these coppery patches in North Carolina's Outer Banks inlets during the spring and fall.

All of us want to have an albacore or a bonito come three feet out of the water, advertising its presence. In the real world, however, anglers are more likely to get less definitive signs. The angler's ability to interpret such signs determines his ability to "see fish."

CASTING WHERE FISH SHOULD BE . . . RIPS AND EDDIES

Even though I would much rather cast in front of a push or into a mud, more often than not I am casting to locations where fish should be. As in fresh water, you must learn to "read" the water. When there is no hatch coming off in a mountain trout stream, anglers know to drift nymphs past logs, undercut banks, and other places where trout are likely to hold. Saltwater fly fishers, whether in open water, near inlets, or along jetties, must learn to pick out the most likely feeding stations based on such things as tide, temperature, and season.

The first thing to remember is that all fish, whether fresh or saltwater, like to expend as little energy as possible locating food. Whether bluefish, albacore, weakfish, ladyfish, jack crevalle, or red drum, all of these fish like to have food served to them. Fortunately, the same "cafeteria" lines that draw fish are often visible to anglers, too. Since much of the ocean is a desert, it is the job of the fly fisher to find the "oases" and feeding stations. This is not as difficult as it sounds.

No term is more important to understand than "rip." From time to time, news reports will announce that there is a dangerous "riptide" at your favorite beach. To a greater or lesser degree, each and every day, on inshore flats, around inlets, and along beaches, there are rips. Every person who has ever been near the ocean has noticed either narrow or broad lines of choppy water moving through areas of calmer water. When a large volume of moving water, caused by tidal action, is forced into a narrow

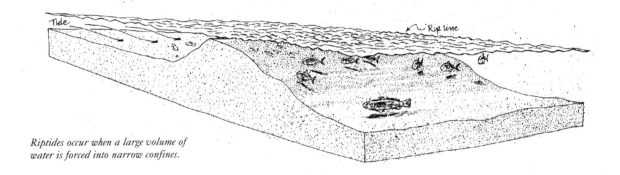

Riptides occur when a large volume of water is forced into narrow confines.

The anglers in this line are fishing a rip near Virginia Beach. Note the "troubled" water directly in front of the anglers. Photograph by Tom Earnhardt

space, the water accelerates, causing a clearly delineated, fast-moving "river." This is a classic rip. When moving tidal currents are deflected by a sandy point or a man-made jetty, water is again channelized, causing it to accelerate, and again creating a rip.

Rips can also be subtle and barely visible. Along virtually every sandy beach there will be an outer bar off the beach. Between the outer bar and the beach there is an area normally referred to as a trough. During low tide it is very easy to see the top of the outer bar and the deeper water of the trough. In all outer bars there will be cuts or breaks. These cuts are significant in that, as the tide falls, they are constricted areas through which water will move more rapidly during the peak flow of a falling tide. Water will actually move down the beach in a horizontal line and be sucked out through the break in the outer bar. This break in the outer bar during falling water will show as a darker area with a heavy chop—another rip.

Rips are cafeteria lines. When water is constricted, the food carried by tidal currents is funneled through a relatively small area. At these points of constriction—the fast-food windows of the ocean—gamefish gather for their meals. Whether you are a

Structure, like these large concrete formations protruding from the surf, almost always hold baitfish . . . and therefore gamefish. Photograph by Tom Earnhardt

boater or a wading angler, you must learn to locate these windows and present a fly in an effective manner (see presentation techniques in chapter 13).

I remember motoring down a stretch of Shackleford Banks, part of Cape Lookout National Seashore, when I noticed a sustained boil two hundred feet off the beach. Because the day was calm and there was very little wave action, I could see a long bar moving parallel to the beach in both directions. The boil was occurring in front of a cut through which water was flowing on the falling tide. I didn't see a bird or any showering minnows, only the small rip created by the outflow. Using a Sink-Tip line with a short leader, I threw "upstream" and across the rip. By throwing the fly into the rip as opposed to "downstream" I gave the fly a chance to sink before I began a slow retrieve across the rip. Over the next hour and a half my partner and I used several different fly patterns and were amazed at the variety of fish we caught—Spanish mackerel, bluefish, an early-season albacore, and several nice flounder. Even though we never saw any real feeding activity, we had, for all practical purposes, anchored our boat at a feeding window and presented flies on sinking lines to predators waiting for an easy meal.

MARSH CREEKS AND UNDERCUTS

Closely related to rips are the marsh creeks that meander through most spartina marshes. When the tide rises, the marsh creeks fill first before water moves into the cordgrass. At these times many fish, both large and small, move into the creeks and the grass to feed. When the tide falls, the creeks, being deeper, help channelize water, creating a fast current. The movement of this current through the marsh creeks pulls and sucks minnows and crustaceans into deeper water where predators wait. I have fished many such marsh-creek mouths over the years and from them have taken a variety of gamefish on a fly. In the southeastern U.S. and along the Gulf Coast, marsh creeks are especially attractive to sea trout and flounder.

In the mid-seventies I was the proud owner of a fourteen-foot flat-bottom fiberglass skiff powered by a short-shaft 9.9 hp motor. In that boat I caught more speckled trout on a fly than I am likely to see in the rest of my lifetime. For one thing, I had little competition in the marshes where I fished, and for another, weakfish populations were not in the distress they are today. Most important, however, I found several locations where, on an outgoing tide, trout would move from nearby deep holes to several small marsh-creek mouths and wait for any crustacean or minnow flushed out of the spartina. Using early bend-back and keel fly patterns, I remember twenty-five-fish days using a 7-weight rod and rarely making a cast longer than thirty feet. For the most part, these were small "summer trout," with the largest fish running little more than two pounds. There, in my small skiff, I learned that fish will come to you if you learn to read the water and get in the right position.

In the chapter on wind and tides (chapter 5), I indicated that they work together. To understand rips, you also have to learn that they are formed by both wind and tide. The more you fish in a particular location, the more you also find that great fishing does not always come with roaring tides and with high-speed rips. Over time, as you explore favorite areas, you may find locations through which smaller volumes of water move that produce your best fishing. Where water drains from a flat covered with grass or oyster bars, as opposed to one covered with sand and mud, you may find that a slight rip or current will be more productive.

READING FLATS

Over the years I have noticed that a significant number of my fly-fishing friends are still dubious about fishing flats away from the tropics. We are all used to reading about, and in some cases visiting, the gin-clear waters of the Keys or places like Christmas Island. Although the flats of the Susquehanna in the upper Chesapeake Bay, the large flats (called shoals) in North Carolina's Pamlico Sound, the oyster-bar-strewn shallows of South Carolina's back country, and the tannin-stained skinny waters of Louisiana's deltas may not come close to matching the water clarity of more tropical locations, they are great locations that are all too often overlooked even by local anglers. A flat is simply any large, shallow expanse of water, whether oceanside, behind a barrier island, or the shallows found near the mouths of coastal rivers.

Compared to rips at the mouth of an inlet or at the end of a jetty, where anglers with all types of tackle gather, flats along the East and Gulf coasts have been, until comparatively recently, neglected waters. I like flats with grass, oysters, and other structures where fish and bait can hide. However, at certain times of the year and at the right time of the day, almost any flat can be productive. Many come alive only at night or during lower light. In the temperate climates of the East and Gulf regions, seasonal temperature changes can determine when a flat is worth fishing. I know of a number of flats, during midsummer and in the dead of winter, that are either too hot or too cold for stripers, yet during late fall and in the spring and early summer, the same locations can be striper magnets.

Flats can be fished in a variety of ways: They can be waded, poled, drifted, and explored with an electric motor. The key to all flats fishing is stealth. Whether in the Keys or in Barnegat Bay, stealth and quiet are critical. Sound travels faster through water than through air. Noisy anglers can "blow" every fish off a flat before they make a single cast.

On the East and Gulf coasts most flats are known for redfish and spotted sea trout. But the exciting thing about a flat is that it can attract a large and even unexpected variety of species. On flats I have caught bluefish, false albacore (hundreds of yards from the nearest deep water), flounder, black drum, and jack crevalle. There have been some real surprises, too. Several years ago, near Harkers Island, North Carolina, I was drifting a three-foot-deep flat, looking for bluefish, when I noticed a disturbance near an oyster bar. As I got closer, I could see the tail of a fish, or a dorsal, flicking the surface, but I still couldn't figure out the critter's identity. The fish stayed in the same location and periodically flashed just under the surface. Finally I saw the black and white bars and was sure that I was looking at spadefish. Even though spadefish are normally found hovering over wrecks and around buoys, I had seen them in the past in shallow waters near inlets. After changing fly patterns two or three times—first a small Clouser Minnow and then some bend backs—I put on a small epoxy crab pattern. I dropped the fly right next to the oyster bar where the spadefish were working and almost immediately had a hookup. The fish was very strong and quickly had me into the first part of my backing. I was delighted, because I had never caught a spadefish on a fly, but when the fish got close to the boat, I could see it wasn't a spadefish. A sheepshead weighing almost seven pounds was an even better surprise. Even though sheepshead are normally caught around jetties and pilings, I have in the past few years caught several more sheepshead in the early summer on tidal flats.

I have become convinced that flats were made by God for fly fishermen. Because the water is shallow, you have to be quiet, and for the most part, the foods found on flats—shrimp, crabs, and various baitfish—can usually be imitated better by flies than by any hard-bodied lures. Also, because a fly rod can deliver delectable delicacies with minimal disturbance, it is the ideal tool with which to fish flats. Don't forget to explore the flats of your area when the light is low or at night. Fishermen in the Northeast have long sought stripers and weakfish in the evening. The snapping or popping sound of weakfish on a calm evening is a sound you will never forget. Almost every coastal area, however, has its own nocturnal feeders, and a small slider, popper, or Deceiver fished in the surface film can work miracles.

Finally, anglers should not forget that flats pose certain dangers, particularly to wading anglers. On even the most uniform flats there are holes or depressions into which a careless angler can slip. If you are wearing waders, always wear a wading belt.

Too many stories abound of duck hunters and surf fishermen who have got into trouble, or even perished, because a pair of waders filled with water. If you don't wear waders, make sure that you wear wading shoes or wading boots that will protect your feet from unseen shells. On my left foot I have a scar, and the evidence of eight stitches, caused by a shell I stepped on while wading barefoot. Whether wading with or without waders, you should always be aware of the tide, incoming or outgoing, and have a planned exit route.

For the boating angler the dangers of flats may not be as great, but there is potential embarrassment. On several occasions (a long time ago, I might add) I became stuck at low tide and had to wait well into the flood tide before I could move again. It goes without saying that unless you are very familiar with the water, never wade or take a boat on a flat at night. If you follow these common sense precautions and observe your favorite flats in different seasons and under certain conditions, they will not only provide you with great sport, they will become a great sanctuary.

In Winchester Cathedral, the patron saint of angling, Izaak Walton, is honored by a stained-glass window on which is written one of his guiding principles: "Study to be quiet." There can be no more effective advice for the modern flats fisherman than the words of Walton, written almost four hundred years ago.

CHAPTER 12

CASTING
The Basics

If you don't learn and practice the basics of fly casting, you will never amount to much as a fly fisherman. It never ceases to amaze me that many anglers new to the sport will drop a ton of money on tackle but spend very little time, and no money at all, on learning how to cast well. I can't count the times that a person having difficulty getting a fly to feeding fish has asked me about getting another rod—as if the rod were the problem.

Like so many other mechanical skills we learn during our lives, good fly-casting technique does not come automatically or naturally. Riding a bicycle, throwing a baseball, hitting a golf ball, or knocking a clay pigeon out of the sky, all require basic coordination and learned technique. The vast majority of people, young and old, have adequate coordination and physical strength to enjoy saltwater fly fishing. Although a great caster can mesmerize a crowd and cause some to believe that fly casting is a form of magic, or at the very least a sport for the talented few, nothing could be further from the truth.

Many people start out more worried about how far they can cast than about learning good technique that will allow them to develop their skills over time. Being able to cast eighty to a hundred feet does give more options and will provide the opportunity to catch more fish. Beginning casters, however, can catch most salty quarry at distances of thirty-five to sixty feet while they improve their skills. There are golfers who regularly shoot in the mid-nineties who love the game. They know that one doesn't have to shoot par golf to enjoy the sport. The same is true in saltwater fly fishing. Although the learning phase may involve some frustration, new fly rodders usually enjoy the process.

I like to think of most freshwater fly fishing, especially trout and pond fishing, as a variation of pitch-and-putt golf. It is a short game, a finesse game. Accuracy and delicacy are most important. Saltwater fly fishing, on the other hand, is like the complete game of golf in which you need to learn not only finesse, but the long power game as well. Although there are exceptions, most saltwater casting is done with rods

The fly rodder in the foreground, Stanley Winborne, has moved his rod through a long arc and maintained a tight loop, both essential elements of long casts with floating and intermediate lines. Also note the slightly higher elevation used to make a longer case.
Photograph by Tom Earnhardt

matched to number 8 lines and heavier. Typical saltwater rods, with their faster actions, are designed to throw larger lines and punch through a wind. Good technique, however, is necessary to get the most out of modern graphite rods.

If you are just beginning the sport or are trying to develop more complete casting skills, I believe there are three things on which you must concentrate. The first is the basic casting stroke, composed of the fore cast, or forward cast, and a backcast that is as good as the forward cast. Not only will you use your backcast as a cast in saltwater fly fishing, but without a good backcast your forward casting stroke will never amount to much. When developing your casting stroke, you will need to use the energy stored in your rod by taking your rod through a longer arc, which is a longer casting stroke. With the most commonly used lines, floaters and intermediates, you must learn to throw a tighter loop as you increase distance and learn to beat the wind.

The second thing that saltwater fly casters must strive for is speed and accuracy. Many of the fish sought in salt water, from bluefish to bonito, give casters a relatively short window of opportunity in which to make the cast. After the target is located, the fly must be delivered with a minimum of false casting. Your first cast should be your best, because with many high-speed critters there may not be a second chance.

Third and finally, successful anglers must learn the casting characteristics of several types of fly lines and know what adjustments to make to cast those lines well. Using Sink-Tips and sinking shooting heads—which are often necessary to fish deep waters and fast currents—is sometimes referred to by casters as "rock on a rope" fly fishing. Because these lines do not feel like, or cast like, ordinary floating and intermediate lines, the fly fisher must always make accommodations. With heavy sinking lines, tight loops are not the way to efficient casting.

THE BASIC CASTING STROKE

Many freshwater fly fishermen know only half a cast: They have never understood the need for, nor developed, a good backcast. Without a good backcast you cannot properly load and get the benefit from any of the graphite rods on the market today. Because a weak backcast means the rod is not properly loaded, the fore cast will lack the speed and authority necessary to deliver larger flies in wind.

If a fly fisher wants to develop a complete casting stroke with a good forward cast and backcast, where does he or she begin? Over the years I have seen countless diagrams illustrating "proper" technique. I have also watched numerous videos (and have even made a couple myself) that attempt to explain the mechanics of a good casting stroke. Books by such casting greats as Lefty Kreh, Ed Jaworowski, Mel Kreiger, and Joan Wulff can be helpful, especially for those who already have some familiarity with the sport. For the beginning caster, however, nothing beats a few good lessons, whether in a group or individually. Although it is possible, with the help of videos and printed material, to become a good caster, a good instructor can save you a tremendous amount of time by identifying faults quickly and helping to correct them. Whether you are self-taught or get professional help, you must then practice your casting skills, just as golfers practice their stroke at a driving range. Casting instruction is often available through tackle shops. Good instruction can also come from a patient guide, but shouldn't you master the basics before hiring a guide at three hundred dollars a day?

In 1972 I had already caught a number of species of fish in salt water on fly tackle, but I was at best an average caster. It was the U.S. Army that gave me the opportunity to improve my casting. I was stationed at Fort Gordon, Georgia, and lived in the BOQ (Bachelor Officers' Quarters). Over grass and at a pond at a nearby golf course, I practiced for several months with both a 9- and a 12-weight rod, especially when the wind was blowing. I can't say that the nation was safer after my army schooling, but I was a much better caster.

Here are the things that I practiced then and still practice today, even though rods have changed from slow fiberglass to fast graphite. First, every cast starts with the tip of the rod almost touching the water. Before the cast is begun, as much slack as possible is taken out of the line. With the rod tip low and all the slack removed, you will begin loading the rod as soon as you begin your backcast. The line should be lifted off the water in a smooth, not jerky, motion, while the caster continues to move the rod backward along a straight line. The forearm is kept straight and wrist unbroken. At the end of the backcast there is a progressive, but rapid, acceleration before the rod is stopped. A fly rod is no more than a flexible lever. By progressively

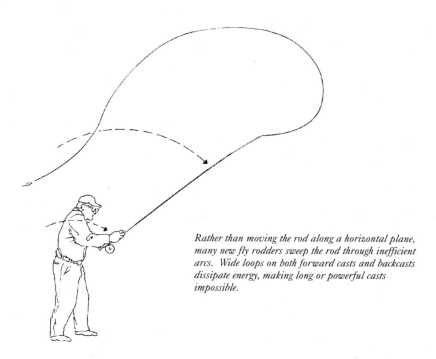

Rather than moving the rod along a horizontal plane, many new fly rodders sweep the rod through inefficient arcs. Wide loops on both forward casts and backcasts dissipate energy, making long or powerful casts impossible.

adding speed at the end of your backcast and then stopping the rod abruptly (speedup and stop), without breaking your wrist, you will have fully loaded the lever and created a tight loop in the fly-line, or tight J with the loop on top. To achieve the tight J or tight loop, the rod hand, and therefore the rod tip, must travel along a straight line from the beginning of the cast to the point where the backcast is stopped abruptly.

Anglers who attempt to cast by drawing an arc or half circle with their rod tip, as opposed to accelerating the rod tip along a straight line at the end of the backcast, will open up the loop. A fat J, or wide loop, will dissipate the energy of the cast. Also, at the end of the backcast, the breaking, or "flopping," of the wrist in an uncontrolled manner will also open up the loop and dissipate much energy. Please note that accomplished casters can often be seen using their wrist to add snap at the end of their casts to increase line speed. Although this is in a sense breaking the wrist, it is much different from "flopping" the wrist. Good casters who use their wrists do so without altering the straight line that must be followed by the rod tip.

The fore cast and the backcast should be mirror images of each other. At the point the rod has been stopped and the backcast has formed a tight J or loop, the forward cast must begin before the backcast has straightened completely. By the time you begin moving the rod tip forward along a straight line, your rod will be flexed, or loaded. As with the backcast the rod should move along a straight line during the forward cast. Again, toward the end of the forward stroke, accelerate before stopping (speed up and stop). Also remember that in making a forward cast, you must avoid making an arc with your rod tip and flopping your wrist. Either will create a fat loop.

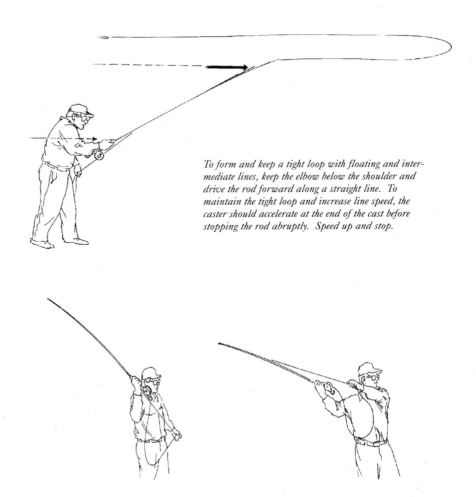

To form and keep a tight loop with floating and intermediate lines, keep the elbow below the shoulder and drive the rod forward along a straight line. To maintain the tight loop and increase line speed, the caster should accelerate at the end of the cast before stopping the rod abruptly. Speed up and stop.

The angler on the left will move his rod through a short plane. The angler on the right, by reaching farther back, will be able to move his rod along a much longer plane for a longer cast. Even though the range through which the rod moves is often referred to as an arc, the rod actually moves along a horizontal line, or plane.

On the forward cast and backcast it is easier to achieve both the straight line and tight loop if you keep your elbow below your shoulder throughout the cast.

Once you have read the preceding material several times and studied the diagrams—practice, practice, practice. Look at your backcast. The loop formed in your backcast should be the same as the loop in your forward cast. You will also discover that the greater the arc (here meaning the distance covered between "stops") through which you move your rod, the more power and line speed your rod will be able to generate. If in trout fishing you have been an eleven o'clock to one o'clock fly caster, you should be able to cast short to moderate distances with tight loops. However, by extending your arm farther forward on the fore cast and farther backward on the backcast, your rod will be able to work to its maximum efficiency, allowing you to make longer casts. The "clock" mentioned above, by which many of us learned to cast, is a good guide, but it can also impose unnecessary restrictions on the saltwater fly caster. There may very well be times when a short, accurate cast could be made with the rod traveling between eleven o'clock to one o'clock. Accomplished saltwater fly casters can stop their rods literally anywhere between nine o'clock and three o'clock (a larger arc of movement) and still maintain a tight loop by moving the rod tip on a level plane during both the fore cast and backcast.

Sometimes it is necessary to throw either your forward cast or backcast at a higher angle. When I am fishing a jetty or an area with brush directly behind me, it is often important to throw a high backcast. As always, my cast begins with the rod tip pointed at the water so the rod will be loaded when I begin the backward sweep. If I take the backcast all the way back to two o'clock or three o'clock, my fly line will be thrown directly into the jetty or the bushes. In such situations you will want to move your rod along a straight line at an angle, stopping your backcast at one o'clock so that your cast will be aimed high. Even though the higher backcast will not allow you to load the rod as completely as you could with a longer arc, you should still be able to make a very adequate forward cast. Another option when there are obstructions behind you is the roll cast, which will be discussed later in this chapter.

The next time you see three or four good fly casters working near each other, watch the angles at which their rods are held in relation to their bodies as they cast. Very few anglers that I know move the rod at a perfect right angle over their head. For the sake of comfort, you will see most anglers holding their rod at a 75- or even 60-degree angle, which keeps the line and the loops off to one side. A good cast can be made with the rod parallel to the water when you need to cast under bushes or a bridge. Regardless of whether you hold the rod directly over your head, at a slight angle, or parallel to the water, nothing changes when it comes to the basic mechanics of the cast. Each must start with tip down and all the slack removed. Some baseball pitchers reach far back behind them and throw the ball with a high overhand motion. Other pitchers deliver a ball with the same velocity using a more sidearm delivery. The same is true with fly casting.

Whether you are making a forward cast or backcast, the direction your rod is pointing when you stop your rod tip will determine where your fly goes. It is not uncommon to see casters making five or six false casts to move the drop point of their fly a short distance from left to right or right to left. With each false cast they change the direction of the previous false cast only a few degrees. More often than not, extra false casting is totally unnecessary because it consumes time, keeps your fly out of the water, and will probably spook the fish you are trying to reach. When you want to change the direction of your cast, simply begin as always, with the tip down and all slack removed. Once the line has been lifted from the surface of the water, stop your rod pointed in the direction that you want the backcast to go. The line will go in the direction the rod tip is pointing when the rod stops. Then make your forward cast, ending with "speed up and stop," with your rod tip pointing in the desired direction. With a little practice casters will find that they can change the direction of their casts with little or no false casting.

The very best fly fishermen use their backcast to deliver the fly on a regular basis with the same skill and ease with which they use their fore cast. There are a number of situations in which you will find that the backcast is the preferred cast. For example,

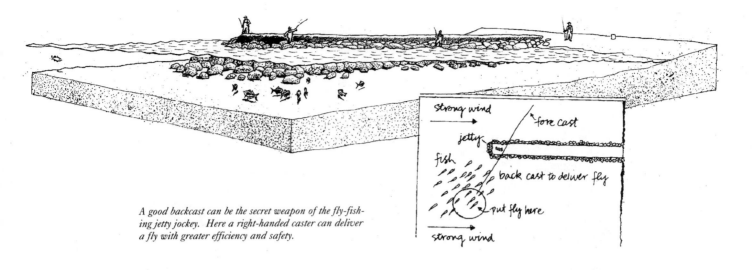

A good backcast can be the secret weapon of the fly-fishing jetty jockey. Here a right-handed caster can deliver a fly with greater efficiency and safety.

if you are standing on the end of a jetty facing into the wind, it can be difficult and even dangerous if you are a right-handed caster trying to use a forward cast to reach fish that are on the left side of the jetty. If you insist on using your forward cast, the wind will blow the fly line and fly on and over you. At the very least, casting will be difficult; at the worst, you will stick yourself. If, however, you turn around and make your forward cast over the jetty, your backcast can be used to reach the fish on the left side of the jetty. Because the wind will be on your left shoulder while you make a forward cast across the jetty, the fly line will blow away from you, making it easier to reach the fish without hooking yourself. In essence, your fore cast becomes your "backcast," and your backcast becomes your delivery cast.

When two fly rodders are fishing from a small boat with casts going in the same general direction, it is often preferable for one to use the forward cast for delivery and the other to use a backcast, especially when they are both right-handed. If both anglers insist on using the forward cast, one of the two casters will always be casting across the center of the boat, making life uneasy for the fishing partner. I once saw New Jersey anglers Bob Popovics and Lance Erwin have a good-natured argument about who was going to get the end of the boat that would allow them to use their backcast. I too enjoy using my backcast for delivery and find that I can cast just as far with almost the same degree of accuracy that I can with a forward cast. You will also find that after a day's fishing you will be more relaxed if you have alternated during the day between using your backcast and forward cast.

THE ROLL CAST

Closely related to the standard cast is the roll cast. A roll cast is an important cast by itself and is the first phase in casting a sinking line (to be discussed later in this chapter). When you want to pick up the fly and drop it back onto the water very quickly, nothing performs this task faster than a roll cast. The cast is also useful when you have a structure such as brush or bridge pilings behind you and it is impossible to make a standard cast.

When casting from boats with outriggers and other obstructions, the author often uses his forward cast to set up his backcast to deliver the fly to locations otherwise inaccessible when using standard casting techniques. In the second frame, note that the rod hand is stopped, pointing in the direction of the cast, as the running line speeds through the guides as it comes up off the deck.
Photograph by Steve Wilson

Here the author again uses his backcast, instead of the forward cast, as his delivery cast. By doing so, he is able to avoid casting across the boat and snagging either the boat's antenna or the angler at the other end of the boat.
Photograph by Captain Norman Miller

The roll cast is very simple. First, just as you did with the standard cast, retrieve as much slack as possible with your rod tip pointing at the water, then slowly raise the rod to a one o'clock position (slightly behind your shoulder, pointing back) and then stop your rod. From the one o'clock position drive the rod forward smartly parallel to the water, with the rod tip pointing in the desired direction. As with the standard cast, stop your rod tip abruptly. This casting motion, beginning at one o'clock and abruptly ending at nine o'clock, will cause your line to roll out of the water and then continue to unroll until it is completely straight before it falls back to the surface. The loading of the rod is caused by the friction of the water holding the line. With practice a roll caster can shoot line fifty feet or more, although shorter presentations are the norm.

Speed Casting by the Clock

Two sets of eyes are better than one. I learned early on in saltwater fly fishing that you must learn the "clock method" to get your fly into the water quickly before opportunity swims past. Although the method is usually practiced in a boat, the clock method can also be used on a beach or in a jetty. Assuming you are fishing from a boat, the bow will always be at twelve o'clock and the stern at six o'clock. Directly off the right side of the boat will be three o'clock, and the left side of the boat, nine o'clock. "Fish ten o'clock, sixty feet, moving to the right." Such a call by your partner

The roll cast is an important saltwater cast and the way to bring a sinking line to the surface. Bring the rod to the one o'clock position and stop before driving it forward smartly. A good roll cast ends with acceleration just before the rod stops. Again, speed up and stop.

should tell you where the fish are and where they are moving. Most important, it tells you which way the fish are looking so that you can place the fly in front of them.

The clock method can be practiced easily on a mowed yard or field. Don't practice over gravel or sand, or you will ruin a fly-line. Place markers around your imaginary boat at various distances to get a feel for twenty-five feet, fifty feet, and seventy feet. You will want to practice casting quickly in any direction, even if it means casting into the wind. That's the way it is on the water, so that's the way you should practice it.

The clock method works best if the angler learns to cast quickly. There is a very easy speed-cast method that can help you deliver a fly in only a few seconds to any point around the clock. First, strip off the amount of line you are likely to use—fifty to seventy feet. Strip onto the deck or into a shooting basket all but thirty feet of the fly line, not including the leader. Using several large, loose coils, hold the thirty feet of fly line and the leader between the thumb and index finger of the hand holding the rod. Your fly should be held at the bend of the hook between the thumb and the index finger of your free hand.

When a fish is spotted, the rod should be snapped away from your body in the opposite direction. When the rod is put in motion, the thumb and index finger of your rod hand should release the loose loops of fly line. As the fly line and leader move away from the body, the fly should be released from its hold between the thumb and index finger of your free hand. Because the line is moving away from your body and rod, it will be possible to load the rod at least partially. With practice a forward cast of forty to fifty feet can be made with no false casts. With no more than one false cast, good casters can deliver the entire fly line to their intended target.

Seconds count in saltwater fly fishing. A school of albacore, striped bass, jack crevalle, or bluefish can be in and out of casting range in the time that it takes to make an extra false cast. The ability to make a quick cast to the right spot often means the difference between success and failure. Guides have told me that their most frustrating moments in saltwater fly fishing have been with clients who were unable to "tell time" and unable to estimate distance—when "fifty feet at three o'clock" meant something entirely different to the angler than it did to the guide. Guides are also frustrated by anglers who would rather have their fly in the air than in the water. The tendency for many fly fishers is to make numerous false casts before ever dropping the line to the water. By the time such anglers actually make a cast, fish such as false albacore are in another zip code.

CHANGING CASTING TECHNIQUE
FOR DIFFERENT FLY LINES AND FLIES

In this chapter you have read a lot about tight loops and speed. There are situations, however, in which tight loops and speed can be a disadvantage. Among the most difficult lines for fly fishers to master are the Sink-Tips and weighted shooting heads. Casters quickly find that tight loops and sinking lines do not go together; such lines can be cast far better with a more open loop. Even though you will lose the picture-perfect tight loop that you get with a floating or intermediate fly line, you will discover that the heavy weight and slender profile of most Sink-Tip and sinking lines will allow you to cast just as far with a larger loop. Fly rodders are often surprised to learn that with sinking, shooting lines most rods can handle at least two weights heavier than the line designated for the rod.

If you are using big poppers and very large, wind-resistant flies like big Deceivers, you will also have better results if you slow the cast down and use a more open loop to present the fly. Because such flies are like big sails, a slower cast, both fore cast and backcast, will allow them to be pulled through air. If you try to use tight loops and high-speed presentations with these flies, you will probably see the whole cast collapse.

The roll cast, as mentioned earlier, is also a very important cast for anglers using sinking lines. With a floating weight-forward line you can easily pick the fly line off the water and begin a new cast. A sinking line or a Sink-Tip line, however, simply offers too much resistance to be lifted from the water with an ordinary backcast. After retrieving a sinking line to a normal beginning casting distance—say, thirty to thirty-five feet—the angler should make a roll cast. The forward momentum of the cast will pull line to the surface and cause it to turn over before falling back to the water. The angler should immediately begin a standard backcast before the line has a chance to sink. When an angler makes a roll cast and then immediately begins a backcast, the surface tension actually helps load the rod, making it easier to cast a heavy, sinking line. A roll cast immediately followed by a standard back cast is often referred to as a "water haul." Unless you master the roll cast, you will find the use of Sink-Tips and full sinking lines very difficult.

As I indicated earlier, in order to be ready for combat on the water, practice is necessary. A half hour every few weeks will help you maintain and sharpen your casting stroke. You can also practice speed and accuracy. For more realism, practice casting into the wind and crosswind. Ponds or rivers are best, but a grassy area will suffice. If you intend to practice roll casting, however, you must do it on water. Water provides the tension on the line needed to perform a roll cast.

A word about safety. Whether you practice over grass or pond, with or without flies, make sure you wear sunglasses or some eye protection. Whenever I teach fly-casting classes, everyone must wear eye protection. Even the end of a fly line, or a leader without a fly, can badly scratch a cornea or do other serious damage.

CHAPTER 13

PRESENTATION IS EVERYTHING

Once learned, a good casting stroke should stay with you, just like any other learned mechanical motion, such as a tennis serve or a golf swing. Casting skills and presentation cannot be separated, but there is a difference. Presentation is both the delivery of the fly to a desired location and the action imparted to the fly by the angler. It is a far more subjective fly-fishing skill than casting. Just because you have the mechanical skills to make a cast does not mean that you know where to place your fly for a given species of fish or how to make that fish eat your fly.

To make a good presentation, you must know not only the habits of your intended target but how the creature you are imitating is supposed to act in the water. It was probably 1988 or 1989 when I began to realize fully how versatile a fly Bob Clouser had created in his Clouser Deep Minnow. Like many anglers with this new, marvelous toy, I was catching lots of different fish with essentially the same fly pattern. One afternoon in the latter part of September, I found myself torn between two options that had been presented to me by friends at a marina. There were a lot of late-season Spanish around, and on a nearby flat some nice speckled trout had begun to appear. Being a real glutton, I went for both. In fairly short order I had caught several respectable Spanish mackerel using a small chartreuse-and-white Clouser Minnow. The Spanish were feeding on glass minnows, so I used a typical fast retrieve, and it worked.

I then ran my sixteen-foot skiff to the grassy flat that had been yielding the speckled trout. Here the chartreuse Clouser failed me, and so did a red-and-white Clouser. I finally decided to switch to a larger, root-beer-colored Clouser (red-brown), believing that it was a good shrimp imitation. I noticed a few boils, and occasionally a few minnows would be blown out of the water by something. After another fifteen minutes I still hadn't had the first strike. All of a sudden it dawned on me that ever since I had arrived in the speckled-trout suburb, I had been using a high-speed retrieve similar to the one I'd used earlier for Spanish mackerel. I knew enough about these speckled trout to know that they were not going to be fooled by a shrimp imitation moving at Mach 1 in a straight line. Having realized what I was doing, I

Varying the speed of retrieve and the angle at which the fly is presented is often much more important than the choice of fly pattern. Here New Jersey angler Bob Popovics works near a sea wall for bass and blues.

slowed down the retrieve significantly and made the fly hop and dart slowly through the grass on the flat. Over the next half hour three specs confirmed that I had made the right decision. By altering my retrieve, which changed the way the fly was being presented to the trout, I gave them something believable, and edible.

As you have probably already gathered, proper presentation applies to targets both seen and unseen. When you have the luxury of seeing your quarry, it is easier to tell how your presentation is being critiqued. Cobia have long been among my favorite inshore big-game fish. A friend of mine from New York had joined me one weekend to try to catch his first cobia on a fly. I had stressed to him the importance of getting the fly beyond and beside the cobia rather than directly in front of the fish. Because of the placement of their eyes, it is easier for cobia to pick up a bait or a fly thrown to the side rather than one dropped directly in front of them. When we finally found a free-swimming fish in calm water just outside the inlet, my friend made a perfect cast by putting the pinfish-colored (green and yellow with barred grizzly sides) Deceiver three feet to the left side of the fish. I had already killed the motor, and there was very little wind. I watched as he made a series of nice ten-inch strips, but I soon realized the cobia was not going to take the fly because something was wrong.

"Strip faster," I shouted. "You're not moving the fly," I told him. In disbelief and with some exasperation, he replied, "I am stripping the fly. What do you mean?"

The cobia turned away at the boat and we never saw it again. What I had noticed was that even though there was no wind, the outgoing tide was moving the boat directly toward the fish. My friend was stripping in the fly line but only fast enough to take out slack. Although the cast was perfect, the fly for all purposes was dead in the water and never moved. I have had the same presentation problem with a variety of fish, including tarpon, redfish, albacore, and stripers. Tide and wind are usually the villains that push you quickly toward fish and make it necessary to strip extra fast to impart movement to the fly. Jersey angler Bob Popovics was fishing at Cape Lookout for false albacore one October. Schools of albacore were staying up, and a stiff wind frequently blew us right into schools of fish. It was a pleasure to watch Bob speed up his retrieve by using a faster double-handed retrieve when the boat was being blown into fish. Again, presentation is everything.

STEALTH

An important part of presentation is delicacy and stealth. Most fish in shallow water will depart if you cast directly over them (lining), or if you even false cast over their location. For fish in very calm water, good presentation may not mean only a delicate placement of the fly but also the use of a lighter fly rod and line. A 6- or 7-weight line will cause far less disturbance on a redfish flat in calm conditions.

Great presentation also means taking into account the angle of the sun. If the sun is directly behind a caster, the shadow of the caster, the rod, or even the line can spook fish.

When approaching a feeding frenzy, many anglers forget that stealth is also important. Streamers or poppers should normally be cast along the edge of the action and not into the middle. Another presentation tactic, however, is to cast a sinking line into the middle of the frenzy and let it sink several seconds before retrieving. Larger fish sometimes stay under the surface action. Whether you cast to the edge or cen-

Watch the angle of the sun when moving into casting position. Throwing shadows with your body or fly line is a sure way to spook fish.

ter of feeding activity, boaters should never run through the school. Stealth in presentation is much more than just the delicate delivery of the fly.

CURRENT DIRECTION

One of the most common mistakes anglers make in presentation is to continue casting in the same location and retrieving in the same direction even though the tide has changed. When anchored in an inlet or at the mouth of a marsh creek during falling water, I have found that one of the least productive casts is straight down current so that you are required to make an upstream retrieve. When mud minnows, shrimp, or small crabs are being moved out with the current, individual minnows or crustaceans rarely swim against the current. Although saltwater fish are more aggressive and not as finicky as freshwater trout, they are not stupid. Schooling baitfish and crustaceans don't normally buck the current. The better position for the caster is to the side of the current flow so that casts can be made up current and across, allowing the fly to be manipulated as it swings across and down.

Anglers must learn to experiment in such situations. Sometimes a swimming baitfish pattern crosscurrent will attract attention, while other times fish may prefer a dead drift. One of the most productive presentations for common weakfish and spotted weakfish is the dead drift of a shrimp or crab pattern in the current, with an occasional twitch. I have taken many weakfish that were simply holding in "feeding stations," waiting for food to be swept to them by the current.

It is important to emphasize that the action imparted to your flies should be done with your stripping hand, with the rod tip in the water. If you try to give action to your fly by moving your rod tip, you will only be setting yourself up for being out of position to strike when a fish takes. (More about hooking in chapter 14.)

WATER TEMPERATURE

Another consideration that drastically affects presentation is water temperature. Along the Mid-Atlantic Coast and the Gulf Coast there are many fish whose feeding habits are significantly affected by rising or falling temperatures. As indicated in the chapter "Learning from 'Heathen,'" the fly rodder should be attuned to the techniques developed by other anglers in dealing with various water temperatures. Falling temperatures may drive some fish out of a particular area, but such fish as stripers, weakfish, and even redfish will simply change their eating habits. Since the midsixties, I have spent several hundred hours anchored near the jetty at Cape Lookout. It is a haven for a variety of fish from April through December. The fish that have made it famous, however, are the speckled trout, which gather in large numbers from mid-October through Thanksgiving. This is one of the places where I regularly use a Sink-Tip or sinking shooting head line to put my fly on the bottom. In this and other locations the choice of line type can be an important part of presentation. Over the years I have caught speckled trout on keel flies, Deceivers, bend backs, and, more recently, Clouser Minnows. At this great sea-trout location nothing is more important than the speed of retrieve, and speed is dictated by water temperature. In mid-October, with water temperature in the mid-sixties, successful anglers usually employ a fairly rapid retrieve that seems to bring out the aggressive nature of the fish. By Thanksgiving, when water temperatures have fallen into the low fifties, baits are moved very slowly along the bottom, and the takes of fish can be much subtler. Again, it should be clear that presentation is far more than a mechanical skill because it must incorporate such factors as current movement, temperature, and line selection.

PRESENTATIONS THAT EXCITE

East Coast anglers know that when big bluefish come ashore in the spring, they are often very skinny and sometimes referred to as "snakes." Fish that weighed sixteen or eighteen pounds in the fall may weigh only ten pounds in the spring.

During the halcyon days in the mid- and late seventies, Joel Arrington and I often looked for schools of "snakes" along shoals and jetties of the North Carolina Outer Banks. Because springtime fish often seem to carry a hangover from winter, they had to be awakened. Joel would often use spinning tackle to throw a large chugging plug with no hooks to get blues excited before we threw flies at them. We soon learned, however, that using a fly-rod popper to excite the fish could also trigger strikes. We would lay out a forty-foot cast near the area holding fish and then almost immediately rip the bug off the water to make a backcast. The popper would then be placed in the same spot and again ripped off the water, making a huge chug. After dropping the popper and ripping it off the water several times, bluefish would get agitated. After three or four false presentations when the popper was taken away, we would drop it onto the water and leave it. Sometimes a simple twitch would induce a strike, while other times the more traditional strip-pop, strip-pop would work.

The same type of excitement presentation—casting and then removing the popper—can be very effective for amberjack and even cobia over wrecks. The fact that a large chunk of "food" is escaping sometimes drives amberjack and cobia into a frenzy. Once the fly is finally left onto the water, there is often a free-for-all. I have practiced this technique over wrecks, using no more than twenty-five feet of fly line and leader. When excited, amberjack and cobia are not boat shy.

SWIMMING CRABS

Like the Deceiver and Clouser Minnow, a new fly comes along every eight or ten years that makes you rethink your game. Crab flies certainly fall into that category. In the early seventies Keys guide Captain Nat Ragland came up with the Puff, one of the first effective crab imitations. The Puff was quickly followed by epoxy flies and crab imitations made of silicone. There are now, however, a large number of very realistic crab patterns, including Del Brown's Merkin, and George Anderson's McCrab. Virtually everywhere fly rodders practice their sport—the New England coast, Florida Keys, Gulf Coast, and more tropical destinations—there are crabs of every size and color: fiddlers, blue crabs, and calico crabs. When I first started using crab patterns, I was not sure how to present them. The first thing I learned was that crab patterns are not good producers when retrieved in steady ten-inch strips, the way one would retrieve a Deceiver or a Surf Candy. Crabs will often swim through the water rapidly for a few feet and then dive to the bottom for the safety of grass or shells. Fish such as redfish and large speckled trout will often take a crab pattern that has been moved a few feet and then allowed to sit still on the bottom.

I sometimes look on the presentation of crab flies as a metaphor for all flies. Unless you have a pretty good idea of how certain prey act, then you will not fool many gamefish. Many of the more generic patterns, like Clouser Minnows and Sea-Ducers, can imitate a number of things if you know what movement or speed should be used.

If you match a great caster against a less competent caster, but one with more experience on the water, always bet on the angler with better presentation skills. Great casting skills are fun to watch, but when it comes to catching fish, presentation is everything.

CHAPTER 14

THE FISH ATE MY FLY
Now What?

Any angler who has fished with more than a few guides has certainly fished with one who feels compelled to yell at eighty decibels, "HIT HIM . . . HIT HIM!"

During those times when I have had such artful instruction, I have usually failed to hook fish and in many cases have broken them off. The exclamation "hit him" not only tends to cause anglers to forget everything they know, but causes them to sweep the rod through a large arc in a single exaggerated motion. This "heave-ho" method of setting a hook has no place in fly fishing.

Hooking and fighting large fish on a fly rod is not something that most anglers do well initially. Many new saltwater fly rodders doubt the capabilities of their tackle and their own ability to land a large fish on a fly rod. In the Florida Keys no one questions a guide who claims that his client caught and released two tarpon in the eighty-pound class during the course of a day's fly fishing. It happens regularly. Until very recently, however, along many areas of the East and Gulf coasts, fly rodders would get looks of skepticism and even disbelief when they announced they had caught a cobia, king mackerel, or even a big bluefish on a fly, especially if there was no carcass to show. Many nonfly rodders still don't have the foggiest notion of what a great hooking and fish-fighting tool a fly rod is when used properly. Modern fly rods equipped with machined reels and smooth drags are capable of taming almost any gamefish in the ocean, except, perhaps, giant billfish and tuna.

A number of years ago I joined a good friend, Steve McDonald, another North Carolinian, on one of his first fly-fishing trips to the Keys. At that point Steve had never caught a tarpon. He had the right tackle and had practiced his casting for weeks before the trip. On the first morning, near Key West, he made an excellent cast and was quickly hooked up to a sixty-pound tarpon. From there things went downhill! After an hour the guide and I were begging him to lean into the fish and fight it harder. At two hours he sensed our exasperation and assured us that he was taxing his fifteen-pound tippet to the max. At three hours Steve was tired of our advice: "It's only a sixty-pound fish and you're putting almost no pressure on it. The fish is playing you."

Between the third and fourth hour the fish swam around the boat, never getting more than forty feet away, and then the hook pulled out. A sixty-pound tarpon on a fly rod is a nice fish but certainly not a remarkable one. What Steve did that is repeated by so many new saltwater fly fishers is treat the fly rod, even a 12 weight, as a fragile instrument that was surely going to break. He also assumed that a fifteen-pound-test tippet, with a breaking strength of one-fourth the weight of the fish he was fighting had to be pampered. McDonald has, since that humble beginning, become an excellent fish fighter and has caught a variety of saltwater heavyweights on fly gear. He now knows the limits of his tackle and how to play a fish hard. Although nothing beats the real thing, the following suggestions should give you more confidence the next time your fly is swimming in harm's way.

HOOKING

Although hooking and fighting a fish, especially in the first thirty seconds of the encounter, are closely related, there are some tips regarding hooking that you should know. For years most of us have watched bait fishermen and trollers use large hooks, 6/0 through 10/0, for such fish as channel bass, king mackerel, cobia, stripers, and big bluefish. In fly fishing, such large hooks are avoided for a number of reasons.

For the large fish just mentioned, experienced anglers rarely use flies tied on hooks larger than 5/0 in size. In fact, most flies used for giant tarpon are tied on 3/0 and 4/0 hooks. Even with very large Deceivers and other large-profile flies, I seldom use hooks larger than 4/0. Larger hooks with their thicker wire are very difficult to set in a tough-mouthed fish, even with a fifteen- or twenty-pound-test leader. Hooks of 4/0 and smaller, with a well-honed point (described in chapter 6), penetrate the bone or tissue in the mouths of very large fish. In fly fishing, large hooks are actually counterproductive. Almost all the flies I use to catch false albacore in the ten- to fifteen-pound range are tied on size-4 and size-2 hooks. I once caught an eighteen-pound king mackerel while fishing for albacore on a size-4 hook. I did not have a wire leader, and fortunately, the fly penetrated the skin on the end of his snout. I was surprised that I had not been cut off by the toothy kingfish, but not at all surprised that a nice king could be landed on such a small hook. The first lesson in hooking fish with a fly rod is to choose well-sharpened hooks that are the right size for the prey imitated by the fly, but small enough to be set in a fish's mouth with fly tackle.

Just as a good cast always begins with the tip close to the water, hook setting also begins with the tip pointed at the fly as you retrieve it with your line hand. Anglers who insist on sweeping the rod through the water with their rod tip, or retrieving the fly with the rod tip pointed high in the air, are rarely in position to strike a fish properly. I repeat, the rod tip should be pointed at the water in the direction of your fly while the line is being retrieved. When the fish takes your fly, it should first be felt with your line hand. You should continue stripping, with your tip down, until all slack is out of the line.

THE JAB STRIKE

At this point the hook-setting motion you use is determined in part by the type of fish and size of the hook. For most small to medium-size fish—stripers, redfish, bonito, mackerel, and so on—the angler should, at the moment the line becomes taut, continue to keep the line tight with the line hand while raising the rod tip smartly two or three times in short, jabbing motions. Since your rod tip is pointed at the fish and your line is tight, you should be able to sink the hook. Also, because the strike motion is a short stroke, the line will not be ripped out of the water and thrown back over your head if you should miss the fish. Using proper hooking technique allows the line to stay in the water even if the hook is pulled free, giving that fish, or another, the chance to take your fly.

If you have your rod pointed skyward when a fish strikes, you will not have a tight line on the fish and you will be able to put only minor pressure on the fish's mouth as you try to set the hook. In such cases, when a strike is missed, it is more difficult to regain control of the line and the retrieve. At the very least there will be lots of slack line.

It is very tempting to sweep the rod tip back when you see a fish flash behind your fly or open its mouth. The disciplined fly fisher, however, keeps the tip down and continues stripping until the fish has taken the fly and is felt with the line hand. You can practice this with another angler in your yard. Cast a line without a hook toward a friend and then begin your retrieve with your tip down. When your companion grabs the line and holds it, note how much pressure you can bring to bear by using several swift, short strikes. Whether you are practicing or actually fishing, make sure you are prepared to release the line from your line hand when the fish surges. The object is not to have a tug-of-war with the fish but to hang on long enough to get in a quick jab or two before getting the fish on the reel.

THE BODY STRIKE

With large, tough fish like tarpon, amberjack, or cobia, a different striking technique should be used at the moment the fish takes the fly and the line is taut. The line should be held tight in the line hand and the body should be rotated, sweeping the rod to one side while keeping the wrist of your rod hand stiff. If possible, the fish should be struck several more times using the power in the butt of the rod and rotating your body to set the hook. Again, however, always be prepared to relax your hold on the line hand if the fish should jump or surge. A short, jabbing strike motion is just not adequate to drive home a large hook in tough-mouthed fish.

THE ROLL-CAST STRIKE

Really cooperative fish will take your fly from the side and swim away from you, giving you instant tight line. However, regardless of what species of fish you are after, there will always be the odd critter that will insist on eating your fly and swimming straight at you. No matter how fast you strip, you cannot get a tight line on such a fish, and it will then spit out your fly. One technique, however, that will take some of these uncooperative fish is the roll-cast strike. If the fish has taken your fly and is swimming toward you, making it impossible to strike with the earlier-mentioned methods, raise your rod tip to one o'clock, then drive the rod tip forward to execute a roll cast (see chapter 12). The weight of the fly line moving away from the fish will often be enough to set the hook and hold it long enough to retrieve slack line so that the fish can be struck again. The roll-cast strike is also a good method when such fish as soft-mouthed weakfish are sipping small shrimp patterns. Rather than using the traditional "tighten up and jab, jab" method, anglers will simply throw a roll cast toward the fish, causing the line to become taut and more often than not hooking the soft-mouthed weaks.

CLEARING THE LINE

Many saltwater fish are capable of taking your fly line and getting you well into your backing. When playing such fish, you must *clear the fly line* from around your feet or out of your shooting basket to get the fish onto the reel. Whether you are fishing for large bluefish, Atlantic bonito, or drum, you will want to glance away from the fish after you have made your initial striking motions and note the position and location of your fly line. As the fish moves away, you must take care that all extra line feeds through the guides cleanly, without loops and knots. One long-recommended method is to make an O with your thumb and index finger, allowing the line to move through the O until the fish has taken all the excess line. I have always held the line with *very light* pressure between my thumb and index finger, applying only the slightest pressure as the fish moves away. By continuing to hold the line lightly, I am able to control the fly line if the fish stops before the slack is removed. If you choose my method, remember not to hold the fly line so tight that the line "hops" and "spurts," making tangles or knots more likely.

Finally, before moving on to actually fighting the fish, there is still one more aspect to hooking once the line has been cleared and the fish is on the reel. Everything I have just described can be regarded as the initial set or the initial hooking. Anglers should look for additional opportunities to set the hook while the fish is relatively close to the boat and not running hard or jumping. After a fish has been hooked, be it a striper, tarpon, or albacore, it will often be disoriented and will, from time to time, stop and shake its head while trying to figure out what's going on. These are good times to reset the hook. Now that you've got the fish onto the reel and the hook firmly set, you are ready to fight it.

FIGHTING FAIR

If you have survived the chaos of hooking and getting the fish onto the reel, you have a good chance of bringing the fish to the gaff, or to be released, if you *concentrate*. Lack of concentration while fighting strong fish is the main reason they are lost. I can think of numerous embarrassing moments when I have looked away from the fish at a guide or fishing companion only to be broken off by a surge or a jump. Even if you concentrate and continue to look at the fish, you must also try to *anticipate* what the fish might do and how to react.

Concentration, anticipation, and reaction are not skills needed only for fighting large, fast fish. A five-pound redfish on a twelve-pound-test leader should never break you off, but I have on occasion been outdueled by redfish. They will rarely get into your backing, but they will zigzag back and forth, taking you through every clump of grass and past every oyster bar in their territory. By closely watching fish, and *concentrating*, you can often lift your rod high so that the line clears obstructions like oyster bars and old pier pilings.

I have hooked lots of cobia and amberjack next to buoys attached to the bottom by cables or chains. Big fish seldom know they have been hooked and will often shake their heads even after you have set the hook hard several times. Once you have hooked a cobia or an amberjack, you need to stay as close to the fish as possible until it is well clear of the buoy and its tether. By staying very close to a hooked fish, you will be able to move the boat left or right in order to follow it around the obstacle. Lack of attention can result in your losing not only a fish, but an entire fly line, to an anchor chain.

To avoid being broken off by an unanticipated jump or surge, you must constantly watch the fish as you work it. When the fish, regardless of the species, is swimming rapidly away, keep your rod tip high until the fish slows down. Once the fish has slowed or stopped, you should begin recovering line as soon as possible with a short, pumping action. Raise the rod smoothly and then quickly reel in line as you lower the rod toward the fish. By using short, fast pumping strokes, you can recover more line than by trying to move the rod through a large arc. Moving the rod in large arcs while pumping can cause you to lose control of the fish; again, short pumps are far more effective. Fly fishermen in both fresh and salt water often forget that the fly reel is not a winch or a pulling device, rather, it is a line-storing instrument. The rod should be used to pull the fish toward you, and the reel should be used only to pick up the slack as the tip is lowered.

Because of stretch in the fly line and backing, the farther a fish gets away from you, the less pressure you can put on it. It is important, therefore, especially for anglers in boats, to close the gap if the fish gets too far away. You do not need to chase a fish or back down on it quickly, but you do need to stay in control by keeping the fish at a reasonable distance during most of the fight.

After initial runs and surges you need to apply as much pressure as possible so that a fish can be worn down quickly. If the fish is swimming to the right, the angler should keep the rod tip low and use a short, pumping action while pulling to the left. Conversely, when the fish changes direction and moves to the left, the rod tip should be kept low and pressure should be applied from the right side. By constantly changing the position of the rod and applying pressure first from one side, then another, you can keep a fish "off balance" and end the fight much faster.

The final phase of the fight occurs when the fly line is back on the reel and the fish is within seventy-five feet. By using your fingertips and pressing the fly line against the rod or cork grip, you can apply tremendous pressure to a fish as you pump. The temptation for a new fly rodder is to "horse" a fish too fast during the last part of the fight. Pressure should be firm and constant, with the angler always anticipating a run, surge, or jump. Red drum, big bluefish, false albacore, cobia, and jacks of

Here the author is putting extra pressure on a fish by keeping the rod low to the water.
Photograph by Lefty Kreh

all types are great close-in brawlers. Patience is required in the last minutes of the fight, because as the fish gets closer there is less room for error.

SETTING THE DRAG

Probably the least understood aspect of fighting a fish with a fly rod is that of drag. Whenever I fish around anglers new to the sport, the question of how tight to set the drag on a fly reel always comes up. Questioners are rarely satisfied, because the answer is not a simple one. The main difference between most freshwater and saltwater fly reels is the quality of the drag mechanism, since the reels themselves are little more than line-collecting devices. Earlier in this book I discussed the sticker shock that many anglers experience when pricing saltwater fly reels. A friend of mine once told me that he had got a very nice saltwater fly reel for one hundred dollars, but the drag had cost him four hundred dollars!

First, you must consider start-up drag: This is the amount of drag it takes for a moving fish to begin turning the spool. Start-up drag pressure is invariably greater than the amount of pressure needed to continue turning the spool. If you've ever tried to push a stalled car, you know that it takes far more effort at the beginning to start the car rolling than it does to keep it rolling. Just as with the stopped car, the inertia of a stopped fly reel must be overcome with greater pressure on the drag, and therefore on the leader, each time the reel is stopped. During the fight, a reel and its drag mechanism will start and stop many times.

Since some reels require less start-up drag pressure than others, the initial setting of the drag will vary from reel to reel. It may take four pounds of pressure to overcome the inertia of some fly reels, while only a pound and a half of pressure will be needed once the reel has been "jump-started." My advice is to set your drag tight enough so that there is enough pressure both to prevent overrun and to apply resistance to a running fish, while at the same time, light enough to allow the stopped spool to rotate without breaking the tippet. Two pounds of start-up pressure is usually about right.

Once you have chosen a drag setting on the fly reel, there is still much more to consider. The object is always to fight a fish with smooth, steady pressure. A large striper, cobia, or tarpon can be landed on a twelve-pound-test tippet if played with steady pressure. The same twelve-pound-test tippet can be broken by a six-pound bonito or bluefish if pressure is halting or jerky. Almost all anglers have heard about "bowing" to a jumping tarpon. Bowing, or simply dropping your rod tip, toward any fish when it jumps or surges helps reduce stress on a tippet.

Fly fishermen should also remember that the reel provides only part of the drag pressure on a fish during a fight. As a fly rod is bent, the friction of the fly line or backing running across ten or more guides also increases drag on a tippet. When a fish runs straight away for a hundred yards or more and then turns sideways and continues to run, a tremendous amount of additional pressure is put on the tippet because of the pressure of the line moving sideways through the water. Fly rodders seeking billfish, tuna, and wahoo often use very short segments of fly line to reduce the large profile of a fly line in the water, thereby reducing drag.

During the fight, especially close in, experienced anglers know how to palm a spool and hold the fly line against the grip to exert maximum pressure on a fish.
Photograph by Tom Earnhardt

Another factor to remember is that with your hands and fingertips you can do much to increase or decrease drag pressure by pressing the fly line itself against the cork grip, or by applying pressure to the spool with your fingertips or your palm "palming." Most of the new-generation saltwater fly reels have exposed or overlapping rim spools to make palming easier.

Finally, just when you thought you understood drag pressure, whether it came from the reel, the line being pulled across the guides, the line being pulled through the water, or pressure applied with the fingers, there is still something else to consider. When going after strong, fast fish, such as false albacore, you have to remember that as backing is stripped off the spool, the diameter of the backing left on the reel gets smaller and pressure on the tippet gets greater. In other words, when a fish first begins its run and the moving spool is full of backing, the drag mechanism will provide the least amount of pressure. Once the fish has taken 150 yards of line, and there is only a small core of backing remaining, the drag pressure exerted by the reel will have increased from two to four times as much, even though the reel's drag setting was never touched. I have heard exasperated fly rodders exclaim, "I didn't touch the drag and it still broke me off. What did I do wrong?" Even if you never touch the drag setting, light tippets can be broken if you aren't aware of increased pressure as the arbor (spool) size shrinks.

RELEASING AND LANDING—TECHNIQUES AND DEVICES

Saturday-morning-television bass fishermen certainly have it easy when it comes to landing and releasing largemouth bass. Bass have a big mouth and no teeth. A firm grasp of the lower jaw is all that is needed to control the fish.

Unfortunately, it is not always that easy in salt water because, on a given day, you may catch several species of fish with entirely different characteristics—sharp teeth, crushers in their mouth, sharp gill rakers, super slipperiness, or tremendous strength. The first decision that must be made is whether the fish is to be kept or released. That choice will dictate what tools, if any, are needed. Although I release the vast majority of all fish I catch in fresh and salt water, I do enjoy eating fresh fish and will, from time to time, keep a king mackerel, dolphin, medium-sized cobia, or bonito for the table.

There are a number of tools available to saltwater anglers, and certainly the most common are nets and gaffs. Ironically, many anglers fail to use either properly. An example that always comes to mind is the day I lost of a fly-rod-hooked striper that easily weighed between twenty-five and thirty pounds. By Cape Cod standards it may not have been a large fish, but in North Carolina waters it was a dream fish. In the mid-1970s I invited a spin-fishing friend on a striper excursion to North Carolina's Albemarle Sound. I was fishing with a four-inch-long Deceiver next to bridge pilings when the fish struck. A half hour later the huge fish was whipped, and we were in open water well away from the bridge. I had a large net in my boat, and I asked my companion to hold it still in the water while I led the fish into it. Instead of holding the net in the water, he turned into Jimmy Connors and swatted at my fish with a fore-hand, then a backhand, then another forehand. "Stop the net. Hold it still," I begged.

In the excitement he failed to net the fish but did manage to snag my fly and pull it out of the fish's mouth. The fish was so tired it could barely swim away. The rest of the day was spent in painful silence. It really wasn't my friend's fault, because good netting and gaffing techniques must be practiced.

I now use only shallow, rubber-coated nylon nets in my boat. Such nets can cradle a large fish without removing it from the water. No matter what net style you use, hold the net still, completely underwater at an angle, and lead the fish into the net. With pliers, fish such as cobia, stripers, red drum, and even amberjack can be released without harm. Old-style knotted nylon nets, with a deep pocket to surround the fish, make releasing more difficult, and uncoated nylon can damage a fish's slime coat and even its gills.

I use a gaff only for fish I intend to keep, and the list of fish on which I use a gaff seems to be getting smaller all the time as I learn new techniques to control fish. In the last few seasons, the only fish on which I have used a gaff have been king mackerel, dolphin, and yellowfin tuna. It is not that I regard gaffing as cruel; I simply believe that there are other, better methods for bringing a fish into the boat without destroying its flesh. If you are going to use a gaff, make sure it has a sharp, triangulated cutting point. I prefer coming across the top of a fish *behind the leader and just behind the gill plates*. It is important to be patient to make sure that the fish is struck when it is not too deep and not too far away from the boat. In gaffing, patience is a virtue, and a good gaffer may pass up several shots at a fish rather than risk snagging the leader or sticking the fish in the wrong place. For anglers new to fish gaffing, I usually suggest that they hold the gaff in the water, point up, while the fish is led over and across the gaff. At the right moment the gaff can be pulled up and into the fish.

Whether you gaff from above or below, the fish should then be thrown into a fish box or cooler in one motion. Gaffed fish such as dolphin and cobia can twist and thrash violently, endangering tackle and limbs. With thin-bodied fish such as mackerel and dolphin, a gaff with a two- or three-inch bite is adequate. For deeper-bodied fish, such as cobia, you will want to choose a gaff with a bite of about four inches. Again, however, you may want to reconsider the use of a gaff for many fish after you have tried the new shallow-coated nets.

For many saltwater fish, including redfish, stripers, albacore, bonito, weakfish, and amberjack, a good pair of heavy cotton gloves, or rubber-coated gloves, is all that is needed. With redfish and amberjack these gloves will allow you to control the fish simply by grabbing the lower jaw. False albacore and bonito have built-in "handles" at their tails. Simply grab these fish at the thin, bony area right in front of the tail, and the fish will stop instantly.

A simple lip gaff is another excellent tool to prevent injury to both angler and fish. They are great for most large fish. Lip gaffs are especially useful when working with toothy fish such as barracuda, bluefish, and king mackerel. I see no reason why anglers should ever keep barracuda and even large bluefish. Small bluefish, under five pounds, are much better eating. Large blues and barracuda are spectacular fly-rod fish that deserve the same care and respect afforded stripers and tarpon. With a little practice lip gaffs are easy to use, since almost all fish have plenty of soft tissue in the lower jaw that can be easily punctured by a gaff without causing injury. If you are fishing for a variety of fish, I would suggest two lip gaffs—one with a smaller-gauge wire hook, with perhaps an inch-and-a-half bite (for stripers, bluefish, small barracuda, and jack crevalle), and a second, heavier-gauge gaff with a three- or four-inch bite (for tarpon and amberjack).

Whether you have used a pair of gloves, shallow net, or lip gaff to subdue a fish, the quicker you can get it back into the water, the better its chances of survival. Even better, try to leave fish in the water while taking out the hook. A pair of pliers is always helpful in removing hooks, especially when they are inside a rough or toothy mouth. Most anglers in fresh water and salt know the traditional method of fish revival. Fish such as redfish, weakfish, and stripers should be held upright and moved back and forth so that water can move through their gills. For some fish, however, the traditional method is simply wrong and can kill the fish! This is especially true for fish in the mackerel and tuna families. If these fish are stopped for extended periods of time, they will simply sink and die. The best way to release a false albacore, bonito, or mackerel is to stop the fish for the shortest possible time, unhook it quickly, and gently lob it headfirst at an angle so that it enters the water with some forward momentum. If you use this method, the survival rate of these fish, and others such as amberjack and jack crevalle, should increase.

Finally, no method of release will work if the fish is fought to the point of total exhaustion and death. I have no problem with anglers seeking records on light tippets—two-, four-, and eight-pound test. What does upset me is when anglers using such light tippets say they are practicing catch-and-release. Use a rod and tippet strength that will allow you to fight a fish quickly if you intend to release it. For years I have used a 10-weight rod and twelve-pound tippet in pursuit of false albacore on the North Carolina Outer Banks. I know that I could catch these eight- to sixteen-pound fish on four-, six-, and eight-pound tippets using 6- or 7-weight rods, but the fight would be unnecessarily long. For these and other species, including stripers, bonito, amberjack, and king mackerel, tiny tippets just don't make sense. Use a rod that will allow you to fight a fish fairly and then release it in good condition.

PART V

FLY FISHING
FROM BOATS AND HOOFING
(MUCKING IT)

CHAPTER 15

FLY-FISHING-FRIENDLY BOATS
And Boats That Eat Fly Lines

There is no universal fly-fishing boat. This should be evident to anyone who looks at the types of water and weather conditions encountered on the East, West, and Gulf coasts. I have fly fished in salt water in everything from a twelve-foot aluminum johnboat to fifty-five-foot custom billfishing boats. With a little ingenuity and practice any boat can be a fly-fishing boat, even one covered with outriggers and antennae. Because no fly-fishing boat is absolutely perfect, I am convinced that you should begin each day with the belief that Murphy's Law applies to the boat on which you are fishing: Whatever can be snagged, looped, wrapped, or caught by a fly line will be.

Because I am convinced that unseen forces on every boat are trying to foul a fly line, I have gone to great lengths over the years to modify each of my boats for fly fishing. I have also found ways to foul-proof the boats of friends and guides in other regions without offending them. Think about any normal boat, with its cleats, rails, antennae, running lights, motor cables, and anchor lines, and you will have only scratched the surface in uncovering the problem characteristics of most boats.

Over the past thirty years one type of boat has stood out above all others as the preeminent fly-fishing boat: the flats boats of the Florida Keys. When Bob Hewes and those who followed him designed shallow-draft boats for bonefish and tarpon fishing, they met the needs of a growing corps of light-tackle anglers. From Miami to the Marquesas, these fifteen- to nineteen-foot shallow-water marvels offer optimum sighting, speed, storage, and a large amount of clean deck space. Virtually all the flats boats also have well-designed rod-storage systems for fly rods. For many fly fishermen they appear to be the perfect marriage of form and function.

Numerous manufacturers now make flats boats, and they have found their way into the waters of the Bahamas and Central America, and in the protected waters of the Gulf Coast, especially the Texas coast. From Charleston, South Carolina, to Hilton Head, there is now a large concentration of flats boats skippered by a new breed of light-tackle/fly-fishing anglers seeking redfish and trout in the magnificent estuaries of the region. Flats boats have also found their way into the rougher waters of North Carolina, the Chesapeake Bay, New Jersey, and New England. Unfortunately, for much of the fishing that I do in the Mid-Atlantic states, flats boats are just not acceptable. Flats boats are for flats! Many of the inlets along the Mid-Atlantic can be exceedingly rough, even with normal tides and moderate winds. Bodies of water such as Chesapeake Bay and North Carolina's Pamlico Sound are, for all practical purposes, large inland seas, and rough weather on such waters can make the use of typical flats boats, with their low freeboard (the distance from the waterline to the top of the gunnel) impractical and even foolhardy. I am completely aware that some manufacturers are now producing twenty-foot boats, with greater freeboard, that have some of the characteristics of the traditional Keys boats, and these are not the boats I am calling "flats boats."

Even when the day starts out "slick calm," it is impossible to predict how it will end. A major problem with most flats boats is that between the fore and aft casting decks there is usually a large, Jacuzzi-sized enclosed area that drains much too slowly if you happen to take a large wave over the bow or stern. Along the North Carolina and Virginia coasts, even the most prudent skippers will bury their bow in a wave from time to time. Wind and weather conditions have therefore made the center console in the seventeen- to twenty-three-foot range the boat of choice for many light-tackle anglers. Most center consoles have significantly more freeboard than the typical flats boat. More important, however, if a wave should break over the bow or stern, center consoles are built so that large quantities of water can run right through the boat and out over the engine mounts. I don't like small boats that trap water in an enclosed area, and the relatively small drains found in the enclosed space of many Keys flats boats do not allow them to drain quickly.

Unfortunately, however, very few center consoles were designed with fly fishing in mind, so many of my most ardent fly-fishing friends and I have had to do a lot of rerigging over the years to make our boats fly-line friendly. First, almost all center consoles on the market are covered with rails, especially around the bow. I have become convinced that some center consoles were actually designed by plumbers because of the incredible amount of stainless steel or aluminum pipe used in their design. Rails grab fly lines! Most center consoles were designed with spin fishermen and live-bait fishermen in mind and do not have dedicated rod-storage space with protective tubes for nine-foot fly rods. There was really no reason for manufacturers of boats along the MidAtlantic to consider fly fishermen, because, until recently, they made up such a small portion of the market. I always get an uneasy feeling when several fly rods and reels, costing several hundred dollars each, are in an unsecured position in an unmodified center console.

Many other rigging features of most boats indicate that manufacturers also forgot to consider the fly rodder. Exposed mooring cleats, hinges, and storage-box lids on most boats can cause problems for fly fishers. The fact remains, however, that for many of the fish I seek and for most of the water I fish in the Mid-Atlantic region, a center console is the most practical boat. Since only a few manufacturers are now building center consoles with the fly fisherman in mind, there are steps you can take to get a fly-line-friendly craft. First, do not buy a boat off the lot. Ask that the high rails commonly wrapped around center consoles be left off completely, and in their

Almost any boat can be made more fly-line friendly with simple things such as a roll of masking tape to cover exposed cleats and latches.
Photograph by Tom Earnhardt

place small, strategically placed handrails should be mounted. Provided you pay the cost difference, most manufacturers will install flush-mounted pop-up cleats at the factory. Small, easily detachable or turn-down antennae for VHF and Loran navigational devices can be installed. Center consoles usually have a large-profile windshield with high grab rails installed on the console. Ask the manufacturer to leave off the windshield and maze of pipes. Replace them with grab rails no higher than six inches. Small rails will allow passengers to stand and hold on in rough water. One of the most comforting changes you can make to most center consoles, however, is the addition of fly-rod storage tubes. I know of several manufacturers that have, on request, installed one- or one-and-a-half-inch PVC tubes to accommodate the tips of fly rods. It is far better to get this done before the deck and hull are joined at the factory than to try to modify a completed boat.

If you already have a boat, there are a number of things that you can do to make it efficient for fly fishing. A roll of wide masking tape is one of the finest things that you can carry on any boat. Masking tape can be used to form a bridge over cleats to keep them from grabbing line. A small strip of masking tape over the corners of storage-lid doors and hinges can also help tame line-grabbing obstacles. One friend of mine who has recently taken up fly fishing still owns an old tri-hull with more exposed battery cables, steering cables, and other line-grabbing protrusions than any boat I have ever seen. He has learned to deal with these goblins by simply covering them up with two old gray wool blankets. Before he starts fishing, he wets down the heavy blankets and spreads them over the obstacles. The same job can be done with an old twine fishnet. No more snags!

Finally, even the worst deck clutter can be overcome with a shooting basket. Also good, but less mobile as you move around a boat, is a plastic trash can or bucket. Just make sure your line lands in your basket or bucket when retrieving.

SPECIALTY BOATS

In the mid-1980s I fished with Bob Clouser on the Susquehanna River. Bob's large, stable aluminum johnboat had spacious casting areas carpeted with indoor/outdoor

Both of the boats shown above are seaworthy, but one is more fly-line friendly. The small grab rails, pop-up cleats, and turned-down antennae of the author's boat, above, make it a safe and fly-fishing-friendly big water boat.
Top photograph by Tom Earnhardt and bottom photograph by Ed Jaworowski

carpet. He had also installed racks on both sides of his boat to protect fly rods and reels. Since then I have seen a number of other anglers with customized aluminum johnboats that are perfect for more protected waters. For redfish, speckled trout, stripers, and even cobia when they are inside the estuary, an aluminum johnboat can be an ideal choice. Not only are such boats good in protected waters, they are also relatively inexpensive, as boats go. A johnboat can also be run with cheaper, smaller outboards than a similar-size V-hull boat that requires more horses.

Another boat growing in popularity with fly rodders is the fiberglass flat-bottomed skiff. Like their aluminum cousins, fiberglass flat-bottomed boats are usually very simple, run with low-horsepower engines, and are easy on the bank account. Over the past several seasons I have fished from a number of these fiberglass johnboats from seventeen to twenty-two feet in length, and I have been impressed with their potential for fly fishermen. These boats draw very little water and are extraordinarily stable, making them great casting platforms. The larger flat-bottomed fiberglass skiffs, more than twenty feet in length, are also remarkably seaworthy. Because of their length they easily "bridge" even a moderate chop and provide a smooth ride. A number of flats fishermen in Texas and in the lowlands of South Carolina have

Large aluminum boats and flat-bottomed fiberglass skiffs have become very popular with fly rodders on the East and Gulf coasts because of their stability, openness, and economy.
Photograph by Tom Earnhardt

In the "no-motor zone" of the Indian River near Kennedy Space Center, canoes have become the boat of choice for many saltwater anglers looking for redfish and sea trout.
Photograph by Lefty Kreh

begun adding poling towers and raised casting platforms to flat-bottomed skiffs. Some of the redfish boats, especially along the Texas coast, have very sophisticated net-lined casting towers, which would make Rube Goldberg proud.

Perhaps the most overlooked craft for protected waters is the canoe. Captain Flip Pallot, when fishing out of Flamingo in the Everglades, would often put a canoe on his flats boat. I have used canoes in North Carolina tidal creeks for redfish and sea trout. In some places, like the "no motor" zone behind Kennedy Space Center, a canoe is the only way to go.

Of all the specialty boats I have seen, none comes close to the "James Bondesque" boats used for redfish in the bayous south of New Orleans. Captain Bubby Rodriguez and others have adapted a long, slender aluminum boat originally used by duck hunters to take fly fishermen across extremely shallow waters to reach creeks and flats holding redfish. The boats are powered by a propeller on a long, slender shaft that looks more like a milk-shake mixer than an outboard motor. The boats, known as mud boats, have been rigged with carpeted forward-casting decks, spotting towers, and rod-storage racks. Captain Rodriguez says that his boats will run "just fine in the morning dew." Necessity truly is the mother of invention.

Among the most unique fly-fishing crafts are the "mud boats" in the bayou country of Louisiana. With their long-shaft Go Devil motors, they can travel in redfish country inaccessible to any other fishing craft except, perhaps, an airboat. Photograph by Captain Bubby Rodriguez

Finally, the newest entry in the specialty market of fly-fishing boats is the catamaran (although a few have been around for years). Boats manufactured under such names as Sea Cat and Glacier Bay are extraordinarily wide and offer lots of clear casting space fore and aft for fly fishers. Captain Norman Miller of Ocracoke, North Carolina, uses a Sea Cat in the choppy waters of Pamlico Sound. He chose the boat not only for its smooth ride but also for its ability to run across shallow shoals and flats. Perhaps the major downside to the cats for most anglers is their cost. The boats themselves are expensive, and all of them need two outboards, though they require less overall horsepower than is necessary to move a similar-sized monohull (V-hull) craft. Oceangoing catamarans have already proved to be seaworthy boats and will in the future be used by more and more nearshore and offshore fly rodders.

NIGHTMARE FLY-FISHING BOATS

As I stated at the beginning of this chapter, any boat can be a fly-fishing boat. Boats with a full cabin, or a smaller cuddy cabin, present special problems for the fly rodder. This is especially true when they are also spouting antennae and outriggers. For a fly fisher on the bow or stern of such boats, the maze is no less daunting than a rhododendron thicket behind a trout fisherman. Fortunately, however, for the savvy anglers such boats offer great fly-fishing opportunities.

For long trips on the water, especially in wet or cold weather, give me a boat with a cabin anytime! Anglers seeking blue water off the Jersey shore and those heading for the Gulf Stream out of Virginia and the Carolinas often have to cover as much as fifty miles on each leg of the trip. In my younger days I made some thirty- and forty-mile runs off the North Carolina Outer Banks in a twenty-foot center console. Even though I and skippers in similar boats always paired up for safety, long trips in a small boat were nothing less than bone jarring. I used to be six foot six inches tall, but now I'm just six foot—too many rough rides. Seriously, a larger, heavier boat will get you to your destination and back in greater comfort and still allow you to practice your fly-rod art. Whether you are fishing inshore or offshore in a larger boat with casting obstructions, you will be able to fish any quadrant if you learn to use a roll cast and your backcast. If you are fishing at the stern of a large boat, you will be looking back at six o'clock. With your backcast traveling along the port side (left) of the boat toward nine o'clock, you should be able to cast to any fish on the starboard side (right) of the boat and behind the boat. Making your fore cast toward three o'clock (starboard side) and using your backcast to deliver the fly, you should be able to cover any fish from six to ten o'clock on the port side of the boat. Use your backcast as a cast!

As I mentioned briefly in an earlier chapter, two methods often used from large boats are chumming and the Judas-fish ploy. Over a wreck or artificial reef, live bait-fish (menhaden, pinfish, or pilchards) or chunks of fresh fish will in time almost always attract some of the larger residents from the structure below. Technically, only chunks or ground fish are considered chum. The fly rodder on the bow or stern will often have help spotting fish from a person standing on the cabin or bridge above. Once an amberjack, king mackerel, cobia, or barracuda is spotted, the caster, using his fore cast or backcast, can then deliver the fly. The trick in chumming is not to "overfeed" fish and at the same time not to let a break in the chum line occur. Closely related to chumming is the use of a live bait on a short line and long pole. The bait is removed when predators arrive. For anglers who think that chumming is an inelegant way of catching fish, they need only experience the variety of fish that can be attracted to a chum line.

Several years ago some friends of mine were chumming offshore for amberjack near the North Carolina-Virginia line. Shortly after the chum slick had been started, fish appeared on cue, but they were not amberjack. They were a school of large yellowfin tuna, which made several passes through the chum slick. Two were hooked on fly tackle and were quickly lost to overmatched tackle and anglers. From the same chum slick several yellowfin in the eighty-pound class were caught on conventional tackle.

My largest dolphin on a fly came as a result of the "Judas technique." During one hot summer day in the mid-1970s, I trolled along a weed line with some angling companions, approximately fifteen miles off the North Carolina coast. The first fish that came to our strip baits was a twenty-pound female dolphin. One of my companions played the dolphin on conventional tackle to within thirty feet of the boat, where we could see a larger, fish moving around the hooked one. Using a sinking line and a green-and-yellow streamer, I made a cast to the side and ten feet beyond the hooked fish. I let the fly sink for a few seconds, and then, on maybe the third strip, I had a solid hookup. Within seconds a bull dolphin weighing just over thirty pounds began the wildest tail-walking display I have ever witnessed. The fish was boated twenty minutes later after two dozen jumps.

In the Mid-Atlantic region and along the Gulf Coast, most crews of large charter boats know very little about fly fishing. Make sure that you check in advance with the captain and the first mate about your desire to use fly tackle. Fishing from a large boat is a team effort, and unless your wishes are approved up front, it can be a difficult trip for everyone. North Carolina writer Joel Arrington once told me an incredible story about a first mate and captain who made life miserable for him and his angling companion, Chico Fernandez. Even though the crew knew well in advance that Arrington and Fernandez wanted to fish for white marlin with fly tackle, they seemed to go out of their way to be uncooperative. In spite of the lack of cooperation, Chico caught the first fly-rod white marlin from North Carolina coastal waters. The year was 1981. Even though times have changed, fly rodders should not assume that all charter captains will welcome them with open arms.

TACTICS ON SCHOOLING FISH

It is a very frustrating experience to be working over schooling fish only to see another boat run right through the school. You may not be able to control the movements of other boats, but you can improve your own luck.

Stripers, false albacore, bluefish, Spanish, and even schooling drum can be approached in deep water with more success if you make your approach at a constant speed. Do not rev your motor—higher rpm's, lower, then higher. Revving makes fish skittish.

Needless to say, never run your boat into a feeding school of fish. Whenever possible get into a position where you are crosswind to the side of a feeding school. If you are completely upwind of a school of fish when you stop your boat, the wind will blow you toward the school, making it much more difficult to get proper movement on your fly. If you stop with wind in your face (downwind), the cast will be more difficult and the fly will sometimes move too fast if the boat is being blown away from the school. A crosswind cast is much easier and will allow better movement on the fly.

In shallow water, especially shallow flats, careless boaters can ruin fishing. A loud motor and a big wake will "blow" drum, sea trout, and most other fish off the flats. A push pole, a trolling motor, or a planned drift (with the help of wind or tide) will give you the silent approach needed in shallow water.

LINE CONTROL AND FAST CASTS

In saltwater fly fishing the ability to make a cast quickly is often critical. Whether you are fishing from an aluminum johnboat, a canoe, a flats boat, a center console, or a fifty-foot cruiser, you cannot make that first good cast unless your fly line is under control. On a windy day fly line on the deck can be blown into obstructions or

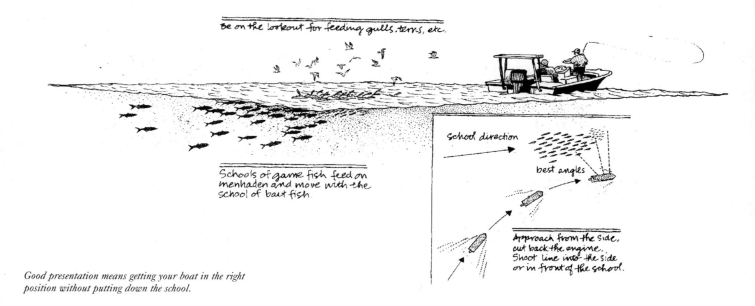

Be on the lookout for feeding gulls, terns, etc.

Schools of game fish feed on menhaden and move with the school of bait fish.

School direction

best angles

Approach from the side, cut back the engine. Shoot line into the side or in front of the school.

Good presentation means getting your boat in the right position without putting down the school.

windrows. A simple line-holding container, such as earlier-mentioned trash cans and shooting baskets, can be useful to make sure your line is ready to cast. Some fly rodders do not like to wear shooting baskets for extended periods of time, and I am one of them. Probably the easiest way to make sure your line is always under control is to use a large plastic bucket or trash can. You can keep the basket from turning over by placing several socks filled with wet sand in the bottom. The amount of line with which you intend to work should be stripped into your plastic container, except for roughly thirty feet, which should be held in the speed cast position described in chapter 12.

If you are using the boat to chase schooling fish, you may find it easier to trail thirty feet of line behind the moving boat rather than try to hold it in your hand. The trailing line is enough to begin your cast, and the rest of your line can be securely stowed away in your casting bucket. When you reach the schooling fish and the motor has been taken out of gear, a cast can often be made without any backcast at all since the rod will already be loaded because of the drag on the line being pulled across the water's surface.

All boats, especially for the fly rodder, are a compromise. With simple things such as a wet blanket, a roll of masking tape, or a plastic bucket, the deck of any boat can be made fly-line friendly. More important, however, is the angler's ability to use a fore cast, backcast, or roll cast to get the fly to the target area quickly. Great fly-fishing boats, like the most advanced fly rods and best fly assortments, are to little avail if the angler has not taken the time to learn and practice the most basic of casts.

CHAPTER 16

SURF, MARSH, AND JETTIES

All anglers should hoof it from time to time. The ability to give chase in a boat and to quickly change locations sometimes causes anglers to forget stealth and thoroughness. When you have only a finite amount of marsh, shoreline, or jetty to fish, you will do a better job.

The other great advantage to fishing on foot is the quiet. Although the surf and the salt marsh have distinctive sounds, they are sounds that allow for thought and reflection. For some reason, when I am fishing on foot, my casting seems to be better, and though they are generally fewer in number, I am more proud of the fish that I catch. Being boatless also causes any fisherman to be a better observer of the creatures in the water, both bait- and gamefish. Anglers in the water feel the effects of tide and currents. Shore-bound anglers have much for which to be thankful.

Two of my most pleasant moments in saltwater fly fishing occurred on the banks. Many years ago Captain Nat Ragland and I were eating breakfast in a restaurant right next to a canal in the Florida Keys. After coffee had been served, but before breakfast arrived, we watched as mullet began erupting right in front of our window. "Jacks," Nat shouted as we ran out of the restaurant. We both grabbed fly rods out of his truck and within a couple of minutes had hooked up right under the dining room window. By the time each of us had landed and released a fifteen-pound jack crevalle, the rest of the school had gone. We left our fly rods with the cashier and returned to our table.

An equally memorable shore-bound event occurred on a trip to New Zealand in 1982. Guide Gary Kemsley had promised that we would catch kahawai on flies as soon as the tide began to rise. A kahawai is a South Pacific critter that looks for all the world like a cross between a bluefish and a bonefish. Kemsley suggested that we wait at a small bar/restaurant across from a large sandbar protruding into the bay. We rigged up two 9-weight rods with floating lines and three-inch Deceiver patterns. We ordered a beer while we waited for the fish to arrive. As the tide rose over the long sandbar, the first school showed up, and, in keeping with his prediction, Gary and I both caught kahawai weighing approximately four pounds. The school disappeared, and Gary suggested that we return to our beverages and wait for the next school. Over the next three hours we walked back and forth across the road several times catching kahawai and then returning to our table at the tavern. There is absolutely nothing uncivilized about fishing on foot.

FLY FISHING THE SURF

On a number of occasions I have been asked if I really believe that fly fishing in the surf along much of the Mid- and South Atlantic region is really productive. New Jersey has some great surf locations, but when compared to the steep, rocky beaches of New England, most beaches farther south are really bland. These beaches, with little slope, can offer excellent fishing if you know what to look for. Just like a trout stream, the coastline will not be productive in all places. As I discussed in chapter 11, you must learn to locate the troughs between outer bars and the beach. Experienced anglers can tell a lot about a beach simply by watching the wave action, but all anglers can benefit from studying the beach at low tide and identifying those areas that are likely to be most productive on the flood. As a teenager, I can remember my father making crude drawings of beaches at low water and even putting small monuments or markers near the dune line. When the tide came in, he was then able to locate holes and breaks in the bar. To this day I still do the same kind of low-tide scouting.

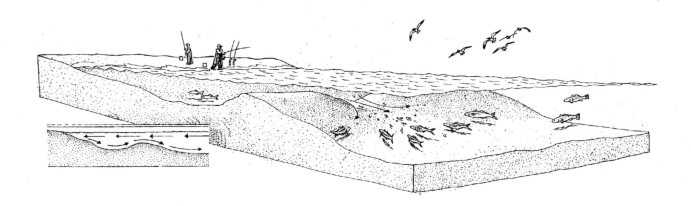

A break in an outer bar can be the site of bait- and gamefish concentrations.

A wide variety of fish are available to fly rodders fishing the surf. Here a false albacore crashes bait in less than three feet of water on the North Carolina Outer Banks. Photograph by Tom Earnhardt

Fly fishing the surf can be frustrating because there are times when fish are beyond the outer bar and well beyond the range of any fly caster. On the other hand, blues, stripers, weakfish, false albacore, and redfish may be feeding only two or three rod lengths away. When the larger glamour fish of the surf are not around, Spanish mackerel, flounder, Florida pompano, and small bluefish can provide great sport on a 6- or 7-weight fly rod. In August and September I have made special trips to Emerald Isle, North Carolina (near Morehead City), to catch three-quarter-pound pompano on tiny weighted orange-and-yellow marabou patterns. Standing in knee-deep water and rarely casting more than thirty feet, I have caught numerous pompano. They fight like a very strong bluegill, but no bluegill can compare to pompano as table fare.

If you are going to be serious about fishing the surf anywhere, there are two important considerations. First, for almost all surf fishing an intermediate or a sinking line is required. In lighter surf an intermediate line will do, but in heavy surf, especially where there are deeper troughs, a sinking line or shooting head is a better choice. Floating lines not only pick up grass and debris, but even moderate surf will roll them up and deposit them at your feet. With a floating line it is almost impossible to make

Saltwater fly-rod quarry do not have to be big and fast to be exciting. One of the author's favorites is the Florida pompano found in the surf from Virginia south during the late summer and early fall. Photograph by Joe Malat

a fly work well in the surf. The second necessity for surf fishing is a shooting basket. Whether you are standing in shin-deep water or waist-deep water, breaking waves and currents will make your life miserable without one (see chapter 10). Shooting baskets also make great "working desks" for changing flies and rigging leaders.

When using a sinking line or an intermediate line, I rarely use heavily weighted flies in the surf. I do, however, use Clouser Minnows in the suds. Let your fly line take the fly under water. Let it pulsate as it moves through the surf or across a deep hole. Vary your retrieves. Don't always use uniform short strips because sometimes a dead drift, with an occasional twitch, can be much more enticing than a high-speed baitfish. The surf can make almost any fly come alive. Sliders and poppers will take a large variety of gamefish in the surf. Even with the surface lures, however, I still use an intermediate line, which will sink just below the surface.

Two pieces of safety equipment are a must for surf fishing. Always wear a wading belt if you are wearing waders. Even the most shallow beaches will often have surprisingly deep holes. Also, it can be dangerous, and it's no fun, to be knocked down by a wave in the surf and have your waders fill up. The second piece of safety equipment, which I can't stress enough, is a good pair of sunglasses during the day and a pair of clear shop glasses during low-light conditions or at night.

If you hook a strong fish in the surf, such as a striper, big bluefish, or jack, it is always best to walk back to the beach to land it. If you're in waist-deep water dodging waves, a large fish is very difficult to handle. A large fish swimming around a wading angler, definitely has the advantage. For the fish's safety and yours, head for the beach. Let the action of the surf help beach the fish.

MARSHES AND TIDAL FLATS

Many anglers don't know much about flats, much less how to fish them. In the minds of some, flats are found only in the tropics, where the water is gin clear and the fish wave their tails. I am firmly convinced that much of the flats fishing, especially on the East Coast, has yet to be discovered. Even where there is significant development, good fishing can exist. Morehead City captain Bill Harris proved this to me in spades one day when he caught a dozen nice red drum in short order, in two feet of water, fishing next to piers of inhabited houses. Some of the best fishing for redfish in Georgia and South Carolina, especially during spring tides, will literally be in the backyards of expensive vacation homes.

A flat can be sixty feet wide or miles across, and some may be wadable only during low-water conditions. Flats can have sand, mud, grass, or shell bottoms. Soft mud or sand can make some flats impossible to wade, so they should be fished from a boat.

Even though the water around you may, at first glance, seem uniform, experienced anglers quickly notice small currents, eddies, and dark spots indicating channels and holes. When you are wading, your low vantage point makes it difficult to see fish that are more than a few feet away; however, the signs of fish—pushes, muds, and showering bait—can be the tip-off.

Flats can be fished with either a floating or an intermediate line. Again, a shooting basket is very helpful. If you are wearing waders, the bootfoot types are best. Wading boots over stocking-type waders seem to fill quickly with sand. If you aren't wearing waders, it's always a good idea to use a wading shoe or a bootee of some kind, to ward off not only cuts from oyster shells but also injury from unseen cans or discarded glass.

Even though the primary targets of most flats fishermen on the East and Gulf coasts are redfish and sea trout, flats can offer a potpourri of species. In addition to the usual targets, I have taken ladyfish, jacks, sheepshead, flounder, bluefish, and stripers. Far and away my favorite North Carolina "flats fish" is the false albacore. I know of several places where they can be caught with regularity in waist-deep water during October and November.

Although more remote flats must often be reached by boat, friends have shared some extraordinary flats with me next to public roads and behind housing developments. One of the most predictable redfish flats I know is at the end of a runway of a small municipal airport. Discover your own flats.

JETTIES AND RIPRAP

In almost every region, especially the Northeast, there are some die-hard anglers who will walk a quarter of a mile out into the ocean atop slick rocks to cast a fly. These strange people are the bungee jumpers of saltwater fly fishing. If you ever stand on the end of a jetty and look back toward land while several waves break over it, you will know exactly what Moses must have felt as he passed between the parted walls of the Red Sea. Jetty fishing is exhilarating and one of the most productive options for land-bound fly rodders. On jetties it is possible to fish for large fish over deeper water than you ever encounter in the surf.

The glamour fish of the Northeast can all be caught from a jetty—stripers, bluefish, false albacore, and bonito. In more southerly waters some of the same fish can be caught, but added to the list are jacks, cobia, Spanish mackerel, and ladyfish.

One of the great things about a jetty is the visibility. As you walk out on a jetty in moderate winds, you will often see the water off-color for the first hundred yards, but growing clearer as you approach deeper water. Anglers also have a higher vantage point from which to spot fish, much like a poling tower on a flats boat.

Jetties, usually made of rocks or chunks of concrete, have nooks and crannies that hold baitfish. Wave action and currents will often concentrate baitfish next to jetties, and there will almost always be currents, or rips, along the sides or the end. Jetties are a dynamic environment for both baitfish and gamefish.

Probably the most common mistake made by anglers fishing a jetty for the first time is to cast a fly or a lure far away from the structure. Start right at your feet and work your fly very close to the rocks. Although fish such as false albacore will often work away from the jetty out of the waves, striped bass and blues may be right in the white water. Because of currents and wave action, floating fly lines can literally be thrown into the rocks. In moderate currents and wave conditions I like an intermediate line. In faster currents and heavier seas, a shooting head or one of the twenty- or thirty-foot Sink-Tips, such as the Jim Teeny Saltwater Series, is my first choice.

I like to fish along as much of a jetty as I can, first fishing close in and parallel to the jetty and then fishing away from it. Since most jetties have to be shared with spin fishermen, fishing large segments of a jetty is sometimes difficult without making lots of enemies. Needless to say, watch your backcast if there are others around you. Because of the currents and eddies that form all along a jetty, fish carefully and slowly. Fast retrieves are often counterproductive. I have at times almost "trolled" by letting my fly hang in the current, pulsating. By all means, however, vary the speed of your retrieves, especially if you have a good idea what type of fish may be working near them. I know of one jetty that produces great spotted-sea-trout fishing in the late fall with the slowest possible retrieve. In the early summer the same jetty is a hot spot for Spanish mackerel, which want a Clouser Minnow moved at Mach 1.

Two items are always required for jetty fishing. First, a shoe that provides good footing is absolutely necessary. Some anglers fish wet, algae-coated rocks with felt-soled shoes only, but shoes with metal studs are far superior. Under no circumstances should anglers fish a jetty with ordinary tennis shoes or bare feet. The odds of injury to body and tackle are just too great. The second item I consider a must is a shooting basket. A forty-dollar fly line will have a short life span if you strip line in and drop it onto the jetty. The cracks and holes in rocks and cement will "eat" fly lines.

Closely related to jetties are highway causeways and bridge abutments faced with riprap. The stones used to hold sand and soil in place also attract baitfish. Tides and wind will cause currents and eddies to form along riprap much in the same way they form along jetties. When driving across causeways, I have a hard time keeping my eyes on the road because of an event that occurred just a few years ago. Early one morning I was crossing a causeway near Morehead City, North Carolina, when I noticed a substantial commotion along the riprap. As soon as I got off the bridge, I stopped the car and trotted back to the excitement. Bluefish in the four-pound range were decimating a pod of baitfish. Within a few minutes I had made the round trip to my station wagon, where a choice of fly tackle was available. I caught a half-dozen fat bluefish in short order. During the interlude drivers of several cars honked and others slowed down to watch. While the action lasted, my only real concern was keeping my backcast away from vehicles on the road behind me. Even though I probably violated several highway statutes and may have created a nuisance on the causeway, I offer this as another example of the many types of shore-based fly-rodding opportunities available in almost every region.

PART VI

HOME SHORES—HOT FISH, HOT SPOTS, AND SEASONS

"You Should'a Been Here Yesterday"

CHAPTER 17

URBAN FLY FISHING
Cape Hatteras to New England

When it comes to fly fishing, I'm greedy. Although I have thousands of miles of shoreline and some two million acres of Pamlico and Albemarle Sound to explore, I still want to sample the bounty of nearby states. Whether I go north or south of North Carolina, there is a cornucopia of fly-fishing opportunity. The more I have fished, the more I have become in awe of both the size and quality of the fishery of the Mid-Atlantic region.

In some ways I feel like the early explorers of the region. In 1524 Giovanni da Verrazano, an Italian sailing for France, discovered the Pamlico Sound and was convinced that he had discovered the "Oriental Sea" and the passage to China. Some sixty years later, in 1584, Sir Arthur Barlow was exploring the same waters of North America on behalf of Englishman Sir Walter Raleigh. Writing about what was most certainly Ocracoke Inlet, Barlow described in his ship's log leaving the Atlantic and passing between large islands into an "ocean to the north." The "ocean" was, again, North Carolina's great Pamlico Sound. Like da Verrazano, Barlow was also convinced he had found the passage to the Orient.

Even after four hundred years, the enormity of the sounds of North Carolina and the larger Chesapeake Bay estuary is hard to comprehend. For fishermen, and especially fly rodders, these waters and others in the region should be appreciated not only for their size but also for their diversity of habitat and species. In a lifetime of fishing, no one is going to master the waters even of his own state, not only because of the size, but also because of the ever-changing nature of the coastal landscape.

NORTH CAROLINA'S OUTER BANKS

I have elected to begin a tour of the Mid-Atlantic region with the waters of North Carolina's Outer Banks. This is an urban fishery because much of the water both inshore and offshore is located just south of a metropolitan area of over a million people. Norfolk / Virginia Beach / Newport News / Hampton Roads is a fast-growing metropolis, and the waters of northeastern North Carolina are local waters much more for the people of Tidewater, Virginia, than for the population centers of North Carolina (Raleigh, Greensboro, and Charlotte) located over two hundred miles away.

The North Carolina Outer Banks actually run from the Virginia border south to Cape Lookout. For the fly fisherman there is almost year-round opportunity in this region. The great capes at Hatteras and Lookout are both considered graveyards of the Atlantic. They are also the dividing line between the colder waters of the Mid-Atlantic Bight and the warmer South Atlantic Bight. The region's year-round temperature is moderated by the presence of the warm Gulf Stream, which comes as close as twenty miles to the barrier islands. Because it is an area where cold-water species and warm-water species meet, the region offers as great a variety of fish as most any on the planet. Along the banks, depending on the season, anglers can expect to find species common to Cape Cod (stripers, bluefish, false albacore, and Atlantic bonito) and fish associated with the more tropical waters of Florida and the Gulf of Mexico (redfish, spotted sea trout, tarpon, cobia, several species of jack, African pompano, Spanish and king mackerel, several species of tuna, and all of the Atlantic billfish). The spartina-rimmed estuaries behind the Outer Banks provide food and nursery areas for many species, and the temperate waters offshore, with their great shoals, currents, and an abundance of food, provide a wintering area for many others.

In the Cape Lookout area the really predictable fishing begins in late April, with weakfish, Spanish mackerel, drum, and the first cobia. In May and June there is a dizzying array of options both inshore and offshore. King mackerel and dolphin may be available both nearshore and offshore. The spring and early summer also bring good concentrations of yellowfin tuna to the offshore waters. The jetty at Cape Lookout is, during October and November, one of the speckled-trout meccas on the East Coast. It is not my favorite fly-fishing area simply because of the number of boats involved. The red-drum fishing in the fall can be outstanding, especially for small- to medium-size fish (up to twenty pounds). The Cape Lookout area is also home to one of the largest concentrations of false albacore found anywhere during October and November. During warm winters they can stay well into January. False albacore in this region in the fifteen- to twenty-pound range are common. There is increasing interest in fly fishing along the southern Outer Banks, and at least one guide, Captain Bill Harris of Morehead City, is a full-time fly-fishing guide pursuing both inshore and offshore species.

The waters of the central and northern Outer Banks can provide even better fishing, if that is possible. Ocracoke Inlet is the entry point for schools of giant red drum (thirty to fifty pounds) during April and May. Even though the wind is always a factor, there are a number of days each spring when these fish are a realistic target for fly rodders. During the summer (from late June to September) the same fish can be found in small schools throughout Pamlico Sound. Although large reds have long been caught on bait and lures, captains such as Norman Miller of Ocracoke are seeking ways to make these large drum a more viable option for fly rodders. Ocracoke Inlet is also the entry point of large pods of tarpon in late June. Like the drum, these fish fan out through Pamlico Sound and are now caught on a regular basis by nonfly rodders from July through September. I am convinced that sinking lines and flies that push water, such as Dan Blanton's Whistler series, will open up the North Carolina tarpon fishery to fly rodders. This is not a clear-water fishery like the Florida Keys, so sight fishing is rarely an option. For fly fishermen willing to put in the hours, however, I am convinced that tarpon and large red drum are more than just a possibility. Chico Fernandez's forty-two-pound five-ounce drum, caught in North Carolina waters, is one of the largest of the species on a fly.

The waters offshore at Ocracoke contain some of the most productive inshore wrecks on the North Carolina coast. African pompano, barracuda, amberjack, and cobia are all options. During the winter, populations of large bluefish are available to cold-weather fly rodders.

A few miles up the coast, Hatteras Inlet and Oregon Inlet offer the shortest run to the Gulf Stream north of Florida. Nearshore, both inlets offer excellent dolphin fishing and wreck fishing. Offshore, yellowfin tuna and all the billfish of the Atlantic are available to the fly rodder. This is not Central America, but there are often concentrations of billfish sufficient to attract the interest of any bluewater fly rodder. I have not caught a billfish off the North Carolina coast, but charter captains have told me that the end of August and the beginning of September offer the greatest concentration of white marlin for the light-tackle angler.

As with most other inlets on the North Carolina Outer Banks, the cobia fishing around the Hatteras and Oregon inlets can be outstanding, especially in early June and then again in September, the major entry and exit times for these fish. Because of the proximity to warm water, both inlets also contain jack crevalle during the summer

No one knows more about Outer Banks speckled-trout fishing with fly tackle than Captain Brian Horsley (on the tower). Shown in the picture is an old hunting club near Oregon Inlet.
Photograph by Tom Earnhardt

months. Both can provide hot fishing for Atlantic bonito and false albacore from mid-September through October.

The central and northern Outer Banks also offer excellent surf- and marsh-fishing options for the wading angler. Spotted weakfish, bluefish, and striped bass are all realistic options, especially in the fall. In the Albemarle Sound behind Oregon Inlet, striped bass have made a remarkable comeback and can be a fly-fishing option almost year-round. Several fly-fishing guides are now available along the northern Outer Banks, but one of the first, and certainly the best fly tier, is Captain Brian Horsley of Kitty Hawk, North Carolina.

THE LOWER CHESAPEAKE BAY

North Carolina's Currituck Sound, beginning just north of Kill Devil Hills, actually runs into Back Bay, the southern end of Virginia Beach. As I mentioned earlier, the area just south of the mouth of the Chesapeake Bay known as Tidewater, Virginia, is now a metropolitan area of well over a million people. With North Carolina's Outer Banks to the south and the Chesapeake Bay to the north, no urban area offers more for the fly rodder. The entrance to the Chesapeake Bay is marked by Cape Henry on the south and Cape Charles on the north. When the mouth of the bay was traversed by the Bay Bridge Tunnel, no one could have anticipated that it would become one of the largest fish habitats in the world. No structure that I know of is home to, or has yielded, more striped bass than the Bay Bridge Tunnel. With the exception of extremely cold weather in late winter months, there are almost always stripers along the bridge's riprap or its pilings. The largest stripers of the year are normally caught around Thanksgiving on the north side of the bridge. I have a number of fly-fishing friends who have caught twenty- to thirty-pound stripers near the bridge's northernmost spans.

The Bay Bridge Tunnel and the mouth of the Chesapeake Bay is by no means a one-fish fishery. Virtually all the fish found along the North Carolina coast also appear at the mouth of the Chesapeake. In June and then again in September the cobia fishing around buoys on both sides of the Bay Bridge can be outstanding for fly fishermen. From May through the fall, bluefish are almost always available. Both species of weakfish present summer and fall options. Nearshore, the Chesapeake Bay Light Tower, which to the uninformed looks just like an oil-drilling platform, is the home to amberjack, Spanish and king mackerel, cobia, and other structure-loving species. Rudee Inlet in the center of Virginia Beach offers access to many of the same fish that are found off North Carolina's Outer Banks. Along with dolphin, billfish, and yellowfin tuna, Rudee Inlet is also the access point for a number of wrecks that hold large bluefish during December. Suffice it to say that few areas offer greater diversity of opportunity than the mouth of the Chesapeake Bay.

THE CHESAPEAKE BAY

Even if you aren't a geography buff, the Chesapeake Bay is an amazing body of water. It is not just a bay, but a bay filled with bays and fed by numerous large rivers, including the James, Potomac, and Susquehanna. Much of the shoreline along its two-hundred-mile length is defined by cordgrass. Unlike Pamlico Sound in North Carolina, where the deepest water is rarely more than twenty feet, there are a number of areas in the bay well over a hundred feet deep. When you look at the thousands of miles of coast-line of its islands, bays, and creeks, it's easy to forget that on the bay and its tributaries are located such major urban centers as Richmond, Washington, and Baltimore. The bay is also rimmed with smaller communities rich in history, including Williamsburg and Annapolis.

For most fly fishermen the bay means stripers and bluefish. Its rivers are with-out question the most productive spawning areas for striped bass. It is believed that many of the large fish caught during the summer in the waters around Cape Cod are from the Chesapeake Bay. Although the fishing is best in April and May and then again in October, there can be good striper fishing in all but the coldest weather.

Although the large schools of chopper blues common in the 1970s and 1980s are gone for the time being, bluefish up to seventeen pounds are still a possibility. Most blues, however, will be less than four pounds. When feeding schools won't show themselves, chumming is a popular way to get blues within fly-casting distance.

On the eastern side of the bay, from the town of Cape Charles to the Maryland line, there is some excellent spotted-sea-trout fishing. Some of the best fishing can be over eelgrass beds that are loaded with small blue crabs. Anglers are usually sur-prised to learn that the largest sea trout listed with the IGFA came from Virginia, a sixteen-pounder caught near the town of Cape Charles in 1978. Once trout are locat-ed, few flies are better than a Clouser Minnow, although fly rodders are starting to experiment with Merkins and other crab patterns. The best fishing for spotted weak-fish begins in May, and good fishing can occur through October.

Coinciding with the arrival of sea trout are the puppy drum, which may be found in much shallower water. A good bet for puppy drum would be shallow, marshy areas between Cape Charles, Virginia, and Crisfield, Maryland, on the eastern side of the bay.

Because of the work of the Chesapeake Bay Foundation and other organizations, much has been done in recent years to rehabilitate this incredible body of water. Catch limits and moratoriums in Maryland and Virginia have brought stripers back in tremendous numbers. Although large fish are a possibility, most are smaller fish from recent spawning classes. There is no better time than the present to catch stripers on a fly rod for anyone who lives near the Chesapeake Bay. There are guide services available from Annapolis, Washington, Norfolk, and other cities on the bay. The size and complexity make it impossible for anyone ever to fully explore, but it's worth a try. A good place to start is with the ADC Chart Book of the Chesapeake Bay (printed in Alexandria, Virginia). The maps are terrific, and there is a complete listing of wildlife-management areas, parks, and marinas.

THE EASTERN SHORE'S OCEAN SIDE—
VIRGINIA, MARYLAND, AND DELAWARE

The northern terminus of the Bay Bridge Tunnel is a land much different from the urban western side of the Chesapeake Bay. U.S. Highway 13 runs past tiny towns on shallow bays and salt marshes. The fishing can be marvelous. Many of the same fish available farther south—the cobia, red drum, and even tarpon—are available during the summer along this wild stretch of Atlantic seaboard. Add to them the seasonal mix of stripers and bluefish, and you have the potential for a great fly-rod fishery. Oyster Bay offers access during the late summer to a concentration of tarpon, which effectively marks the north end of their migration. One day several years ago, outdoor writer Bob Hutchinson and angler Vic Gaspeny hooked four tarpon on fly tackle near Oyster Bay. Neither Hutchinson nor any other expert on the region believes that there will ever be predictable fly-rod opportunities for tarpon, cobia, or king mackerel in the same way that there are for striped bass, blues, and weakfish, but even the possibility of such fish on a fly is exciting. Fly rodders will learn much more about nearshore waters, surf, and marsh from Cape Charles to Ocean City, Maryland, in the years to come. Like many other areas, it is by no means an unexplored fishery, rather, it is a fishery with great fly-rod potential.

DELAWARE BAY AND THE JERSEY SHORE

I first learned about the Delaware Bay fishery in 1972. At that time the Saltwater Fly Rodders of America (SWFA) made its headquarters at Cape May Courthouse, New Jersey, at the northern entrance to the bay. Like other areas in the Mid-Atlantic region, the big three were stripers, bluefish, and common weakfish—but what weakfish! It was in the seventies and early eighties that the Delaware Bay produced double-digit grays for fly rodders using sinking lines. The large grays are gone, at least for the time being, but bass and bluefish are still an option.

No area of the Atlantic seaboard epitomizes urban fly-rod opportunities better than the coastline of New Jersey. Only a little more than a hundred miles long from top to bottom, the Jersey shore is packed with fly-fishing opportunities and is one of saltwater fly-fishing's fastest-growing regions. Two of the area's most accomplished fly rodders, Bob Popovics (Seaside Park, New Jersey) and Ed Jaworowski (Philadelphia), have been among the most instrumental in the region's evolution toward fly fishing. Jaworowski told me about arriving at one of his favorite Jersey surf-fishing locations only to find seventeen other fly fishermen there before him. Seventeen fly rodders in the surf anywhere is an amazing number! Popovics, a restaurateur, is known in the region for both his epoxy flies and his spaghetti sauce. In Seaside Park, midway between New York and Atlantic City, Popovics served spaghetti to a number of fly-fishing friends at informal get-togethers. That informal group later became the Atlantic Saltwater Fly Rodders, a club with almost two hundred active members.

Probably the most famous locations along the Jersey shore are the Toms River/ Barnegat Bay area, Great Bay, and Shark River. New Jersey has excellent opportunities for fly rodders in the bays behind barrier islands, from its numerous jetties, nearshore and offshore. The stripers show up in mid-April along with the Boston mackerel. The bluefish follow in mid-May. Atlantic bonito are basically nearshore fish (four to seven miles offshore) and arrive in July. False albacore are more obliging for surf and jetty fishermen and come to play from mid-August to October. Even though stripers, blues, and false albacore are the big three, as they are in most of the Mid-Atlantic and Northeast, anglers of the region have been smart to explore fly-rod

*Jetties can provide some of the most exciting fishing for shore-bound anglers. Here photographer Ed Jaworowski
captures fly-fishing drama on a New Jersey jetty.* Photograph by Ed Jaworowski

opportunities for less glamorous quarry. Beginning in April, a number of fly rodders
target Boston mackerel, which can be found from three to eighteen miles offshore.
Even though these fish are rarely over three pounds, they are great sport on small
Clousers and Candies. Summer flounder (fluke) come into the bays in July, but the
largest of the species are caught in September. Perhaps the most sought-after
nonglamour fish is the common weakfish, which is found along edges in seven feet
of water inside the bays. They are best caught on sinking lines such as the Teeny
T350 with Clouser Minnows.

White perch, although not as popular as their glamorous striper cousins, provide great sport on light (6- and 7-weight) rods.
Photo by Ed Jaworowski

Another small fish that produces a lot of excitement in New Jersey are the white perch, which are found well back in the estuaries in spring and fall. They can even be taken in the winter during warm spells, and fish of two pounds are quite common for fly rodders. Small Clousers and even Crazy Charlie patterns (bonefish flies) are good perch producers.

Many southern anglers are surprised to learn that dolphin are caught well inside the Gulf Stream off the Jersey shore during late summer months. Although most of the fish are "shingles" weighing three to five pounds, they make great fly-rod targets for big-city anglers. Farther offshore, white marlin and big yellowfin tuna are a possibility for bluewater anglers. Several very large yellowfin have been caught by fly fishermen launching from New Jersey ports.

NEW YORK TO MASSACHUSETTS

There is not a saltwater fly fisherman around who has not seen photographs of large bluefish and nice stripers in the hands of fly rodders beside the Statue of Liberty, in front of the World Trade Center, or in the East River. Even though New York Harbor is a high-crime area, blues and bass do venture into New York waters in late spring and remain an option for Big Apple anglers until late in the year. This is mostly a shooting head/deepwater fishery, but if you can catch ten-pound blues and bass on a fly near your office, who cares! Farther north there is also fly-rod opportunity for bass, bluefish, fluke, and weaks in Long Island Sound.

The really great fishery of the Northeast, and one of the best on the East Coast, begins at Montauk and includes Block Island and the waters around Rhode Island, Martha's Vineyard, Nantucket, and Cape Cod. The region is a hotbed of fly fishing, with good guide services available for outsiders like me. The fish and techniques of the area have been exquisitely chronicled by Lou Tabory in *Inshore Fly Fishing*. Suffice it to say that the rocky shores and steep beaches offer the East Coast's best habitat for stripers, bluefish, Atlantic bonito, and false albacore. The fishery is a little later than the Jersey fishery farther south, and bass and bluefish can be expected to arrive sometime in June and remain until the cold winds of October. False albacore and bonito arrive in the late summer and depart the area during the first part of October.

Anglers who are used to Florida Keys fishing can hop onto the Hewes flats craft belonging to Portsmouth, Rhode Island, guide Mike Kenfield, or similar craft belonging to other guides of the region, and just pretend there are mangroves and palm trees. There is no pretending, however, when New England "bonefish," bonito, or false albacore rip off a hundred yards of backing. This great fishery at the top of the Mid-Atlantic Bight has a relatively short season, but few areas can match its quality.

CHAPTER 18

THE SOUTHERN FISHERY
Cape Fear to the Gulf States

The craze several years ago at trendy restaurants was "blackened redfish." Restaurants across the country were serving redfish fillets coated with pepper and hot spices, then charred on both sides in the hottest possible skillet. The recipe and technique were developed by famous New Orleans chef Paul Prudhomme. No one could have anticipated the commercial pressure put on redfish everywhere to meet restaurant demands for the dish. It has been said many times that Prudhomme almost single-handedly wiped out the southern redfish population. The irony is that Prudhomme used the hot spices and charring technique on almost any fish flesh that needed help masking its inadequacies. Even though an old raincoat coated with pepper and seared at 500 degrees could have probably been made edible using his technique, it was the poor redfish that the culinary world targeted for extinction.

Fortunately, much has happened in virtually all southern waters holding redfish to improve their numbers. Many states have banned inshore netting and imposed catch limits. For fly fishermen along southeastern shores and the Gulf of Mexico, this is great news, because there is no better or more predictable fly-fishing quarry than redfish. A close second in popularity among fly rodders is the spotted sea trout, known in most southern locales as speckled trout. I decided to combine an exploration of the fisheries of the Southeast and the Gulf Coast because they are so very similar, both in available species and in the techniques used to catch them.

SOUTHEASTERN NORTH CAROLINA COAST TO GEORGIA

As you leave the southern end of the North Carolina Outer Banks at Cape Lookout, you will notice that the coast begins to head in a southwesterly direction almost all the way to the Florida line. Along this entire stretch of coast there are barrier islands covered with live oaks and palmetto palms. The palms begin at Cape Fear, North Carolina, and mark the beginning of a semitropical fishery in the South Atlantic

The historic homes of Charleston's Battery district provide a spectacular backdrop for fly fishing in Charleston Harbor. Here Captain Mike Able is waiting for jack crevalle to surface.
Photograph by Tom Earnhardt

Bight. Although the Gulf Stream is well away from the mainland, from southeastern North Carolina to Georgia, there is phenomenal inshore and offshore fishing for fly rodders. For reasons related to the concave shape of the coastline, the tides begin to get larger as you leave Wilmington, North Carolina, and head south. The average four- and five-foot tides of North Carolina become seven feet around Charleston. At the deepest indentation of the coast at St. Simons Island near Brunswick, Georgia, tides will average close to nine feet.

Along this entire region of coastline the number-one inshore fish for fly rodders is the redfish, also known as spottail bass in much of South Carolina and Georgia. Redfish are most predictable along the southeastern coast from late April through November. In moderate winters the fishery can be almost year-round. Such guides as Captains Mike Able and Jerry Ciandella in the Charleston area, and Captain Fuzzy Davis of Hilton Head, have done more than perhaps any other guides to develop inshore fisheries for fly rodders. They were the pioneers, and there are now excellent guides from Wilmington, North Carolina, to Brunswick, Georgia.

Using Keys-type flats boats, guides look for schools of redfish during the first part of the incoming tide and the last part of falling water. These times are critical

Here angler Jack Golden shows a great fly-rod catch, a thirty-pound jack crevalle taken on a popper in Charleston Harbor.
Photograph by Captain Jerry Ciandella

because the large tidal changes make it almost impossible to spot schools once flats have been covered by five or more feet of water. During the summer months the water in which reds are found is often quite muddy because of the presence of mullet schools and lots of shrimp. Pushes and wakes, sometimes marked by seagulls, often betray moving pods of redfish. Fish can normally be found working the edges of oyster bars and spartina marshes. Popular flies for these fish are bend backs, Dahlberg Divers, and Clouser Minnows.

The higher tides during the full moon and new moon each month allow redfish to move into areas normally inaccessible to them—the fiddler-crab flats. In water sometimes less than a foot deep, redfish will literally stand on their heads trying to get at their twice-a-month crab treats. To take advantage of the fiddler frenzy, you will need to use a Merkin or a McCrab.

During the same season spotted weakfish can also be taken from the marsh creeks along the southeast coast. Unlike the redfish, however, speckled-trout fishing is, for the most part, blind casting with Clouser Minnows or bend backs. Many fly rodders prospect with plastic grubs or live shrimp, using spinning gear until a concentration is found, before breaking out their number-8 outfits, the same fly rod used for redfish.

There are other great inshore fly-rod options. Beaufort, South Carolina, has long been known for its great cobia fishing, but virtually every inlet in the region is used by cobia in the early spring and then again during their departure in early fall. Buoy-circling cobia and cobia following a bait-hooked buddy are the easiest targets for fly rodders.

A remarkable fishery has developed in Charleston Harbor and in other areas of the Southeast for jack crevalle. From June through Labor Day, jacks school up and move around inside protected areas. If they aren't exploding under baitfish, they can be spotted either by a push of water or by a telltale fin protruding from the water. Poppers on 3/0 hooks are the best choice, followed by large Deceivers. Jacks in the region can weigh well over thirty pounds, so a shock tippet of thirty- to fifty-pound monofilament is suggested. Also inside harbors and bays during the summer months are ladyfish, bluefish, and Spanish mackerel. Bluefish and Spanish are best taken on Clouser Minnows, while ladyfish will take both Clousers and poppers. Use a thirty-pound shock tippet for the "ladies."

From North Carolina to Georgia, there is an excellent nearshore and offshore fishery. Again, the most predictable fish, and certainly the easiest to catch, are dolphin, which hang out under sargassum mats. Sea-Ducers, Deceivers, and Clousers will all take dolphin. In nice weather try blind casting for dolphin under floating sargassum or debris, and keep a sharp eye out for tripletail, a very underrated fly-rod target. Larger bonefish patterns, like Crazy Charlies, are good flies for tripletail. One captain in north Florida recently lamented in a half-joking observation that tripletail fishing used to be better when there was more trash in the water: "You conservationists have got things too clean! Tripletail hide under trash."

The artificial reefs of the region are, during the summer, home to amberjack, cobia, and barracuda, all of which are great fly-rod fish. Jacks and cobia do require a heavier rod and a fifty-pound shock tippet. If you have never caught a barracuda on a fly, you are in for a real treat. Although the fight is not long, their speed and jumping ability will astonish you. A long, braided needlefish fly on a short, solid wire tippet is standard fare for cuda.

With redfish almost year-round, and an excellent seasonal variety of inshore and offshore species, not only does the Southeast have a fishery that should excite locals, but it is a fishery that deserves to become a destination for fly rodders from across the nation. Golfers should consider carrying a four-piece rod in their bags, since many swanky barrier-island golf courses are next to fiddler-crab flats!

Along the Southeastern U. S. and the Gulf Coast, dolphin rarely disappoint offshore when conditions are right.
Photograph by Joel Arrington

WHERE THE SPARTINA ENDS . . . FLORIDA'S INDIAN RIVER

If you have never taken a close look at Florida's Atlantic coastline, then you would not know that Florida's Indian River system actually includes a significant portion of central Florida's east coast. That system, which also includes Mosquito Lagoon and Banana River, is almost 150 miles long and has its southern terminus at Jupiter Inlet. For the fly fisherman there is a smorgasbord of opportunity, including ladyfish, snook, jack crevalle, and tarpon. The money fish in the lagoon, however, are the big redfish and sea trout available to anglers with boats and to those who like to wade. Although most redfish are under ten pounds, fish of over forty pounds have been caught in the Indian River. Spotted sea trout have long been a major draw, and specs in excess of ten pounds were quite common a few years ago. Although the claim of "sea trout capital" might be challenged by Texas anglers, there is still phenomenal speckled-trout fishing available to fly rodders. Bend backs and Clouser Minnows are good choices

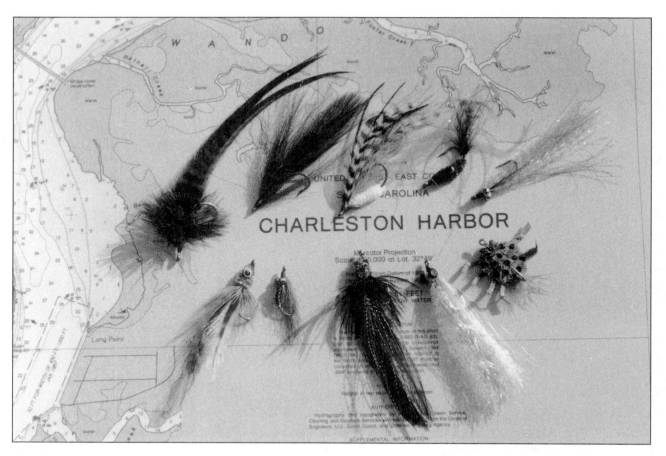

From Georgetown, South Carolina, to Savannah, Georgia, there is a wide variety of inshore fish for fly rodders, including redfish, speckled trout, ladyfish, and jack crevalle. Shown here are some of the favorite flies of Captain Jerry Ciandella, one of the Low Country's best skiff guides. Photograph by Captain Jerry Ciandella

The great Indian River estuary marks the southern boundary of the spartina ecosystems and the beginning of the mangroves. These waters provide numerous options for fly fishers almost year-round.
Photograph by Captain Jon Cave

for both reds and trout, but the thick grass preferred by both species has caused many fly rodders to go to deerhair sliders, poppers, and foam divers.

There is an excellent guide corps for light-tackle fishermen, who can show clients a number of options. Captains Jon Cave and Dennis Hammond are among a number of guides in the region who are both innovative fly tiers and anglers. One interesting option is in the Titusville area across from Kennedy Space Center. In this area you may want to consider fishing the "no motor" zone, or canoe water, which receives far less fishing pressure than the areas open to motorized boats.

Offshore, the possibilities for fly rodders are almost limitless. Jack crevalle, king mackerel, dolphin, and a variety of other large fish are available relatively close to shore. Fly fishers wanting a billfish should not forget about Stuart, Florida, and its world-class sailfish reputation.

For new fly rodders wanting variety and action, few places can compete with the Indian River system. On my last trip to Orlando, I again passed up the opportunity to meet Mickey Mouse and headed for the lagoons.

THE GULF COAST HAS IT ALL

Not too long ago I was invited to fish in Louisiana waters with an experienced fly rodder. When I asked what our options were, he provided a list of both fish and places longer than the combined menu-and-wine list of a New Orleans restaurant. In the marsh, redfish, trout, and even black drum were a possibility. Inshore there were lemon fish (cobia) and jack crevalle. The offshore oil rigs held more lemon fish, king mackerel, amberjack, and bonito. There was bluewater fishing, too, for a variety of species. If you happen to live on or near the Gulf Coast, Florida, Alabama, Mississippi, Louisiana, and Texas, and have never taken your fly rod to the brine, then you are missing some of the best saltwater fly fishing in America today.

As indicated earlier, the redfish have made a phenomenal comeback, and they are available on flats and in deep water from the west coast of Florida to Texas. Lunar/solar tides along the Gulf Coast are generally less than a foot and a half, so wind tides often have the greatest effect on fishing. Wind-driven water is especially significant in Texas, where the wind can make a flat too deep or just right. The more traditional bend back patterns and Clouser Minnows are always good choices, but Gulf redfish also like deerhair sliders and Dahlberg Divers. Local favorites, especially in the Louisiana marshes, include spoon flies and flies tied with a rattle cartridge. The spoon flies are the fly-fishing equivalent of the Johnson Gold Spoon, long the favorite redfish lure of the spin fisherman.

If you want to see some real innovation in shallow-water technology, then you should check out the rigs used by guides in Texas and Louisiana. In Texas many of the boats use fiberglass "sleds"—wide, flat-bottomed boats that draw almost no water. As has already been mentioned in the chapter on boating, Louisiana Captain Bubby Rodriguez and his partners use "mud boats" with long-shaft Go Devil motors. With the exception of airboats, no craft draws less water than a mud boat.

The Gulf Coast also boasts some of the best speckled-trout flats anywhere. Even though the Indian River fishery of Florida can produce monster trout, Texans also have a legitimate claim to being the spec capital of the world. In the temperate cli-

In October and November, the Gulf Coast offers some of the best fly-rod flounder fishing available.
Photograph by Captain Jerry Ciandella

mate of the Gulf area, trout can be caught on flies virtually year-round, with the best times being mid-April through May and then again in the early fall. Many of the same flies used for redfish (bend backs, Dahlbergs, and sliders) will catch specs, but you should also carry a good shrimp pattern, some poppers, and several different colors of Sea-Ducers. Many of the Texas flats have names with a Spanish flair, such as Laguna Madre and Padre Island. While most fishing is done from shallow-water boats, wading is also possible and productive in many areas.

Although the redfish and the specs get most of the press in the Gulf states, great flounder fishing is also a possibility, especially during October and November, when they are heading out of the estuaries. Although most are caught by fly rodders targeting other species, flounder should not be overlooked, since they are both great gamefish and excellent table fare. The deerhair sliders, Clousers, and even poppers used for specs and redfish will also take flatties.

FISH IN "THEM THAR" RIGS

Along the southeastern U.S. coast there is not much structure inshore except for ships put there by acts of God, and man-made artificial reefs. On the Gulf Coast, however, there are literally hundreds of oil rigs that produce more than crude oil. Each oil rig, with its barnacle-covered pilings, has its own ecosystem. When there are several oil rigs together, the fish-attracting possibilities can be even greater. Many rigs are located within twenty miles of the coast, making them accessible to center-console anglers. King mackerel, cobia, and amberjack are the fish that usually come to mind when anglers think of these nearshore structures. The Gulf rigs, however, contain these and many more, including bonito, jack crevalle, Spanish mackerel, dolphin, and even big redfish (called bull drum on the Gulf Coast). The deepwater rigs farther offshore hold wahoo and tuna (yellowfin and blackfin). Needless to say, this is not light-tackle territory unless you are targeting Spanish mackerel and bonito. 11- and 12-weight fly rods are necessary for the bigger flies and fish and because greater lifting power is needed in deep water. Although fish can sometimes be taken on the surface with floating or intermediate lines, sinking lines or shooting heads are often necessary. Even if personal safety were not a factor, fishing right next to oil rigs can mean a lost fly line. It is therefore necessary sometimes to chum or use live baitfish to pull large fish away from their metal fortresses.

As I stated earlier in this book, old habits die hard. After generations of anglers have fished the southeast and Gulf coasts from big boats using stout rods, it is won-

Light towers and drilling platforms can be the ticket to great nearshore/offshore fishing.

derful now to see a new generation of light-tackle anglers pursuing the same fish with gear that better allows fish to display their fighting skills. At the head of the class of light-tackle anglers is an ever-growing number of fly fishermen who have both the skill and the equipment to pursue almost any fish in the ocean.

The great fisheries in the Keys, Bahamas, and numerous other warm-water destinations will always be special to saltwater fly fishermen, and they will remain dream destinations. Most fly fishing, however, will be done by anglers in their home waters. Fly fishermen tend to work closer to their quarry, and more than any other group practice catch-and-release. They are also more vocal about conservation matters. Because of the activism of growing numbers of fly fishermen in all coastal regions, stressed fisheries will have a better chance of recovery.

From urban areas to uninhabited, windswept barrier islands, fly fishing has brought new angling enjoyment to thousands who would have never considered using a long rod in the salt only a few years ago. Welcome to angling's quiet revolution.

PARTING NOTES ON ETIQUETTE

Miss Manners Got Run Over by a Center Console

There are few uncrowded areas along America's coastline. Fly rodders—in fact, all anglers—must share the same water with Jet Skis, sailboats, commercial fishing boats, and thousands of pleasure boats. There are so many boats in coastal communities that they are often stored, mausoleum-style, six or seven high in large dry-stack buildings. Beaches that would be productive fishing areas are, for all practical purposes, off-limits during the summer because of crowds of bathers and swimmers. Too often the mix of competing uses in our nation's waters is not a happy one. I have lost fly lines to speeding boats even when fishing well away from congested areas and have watched schools of fish run over by boaters oblivious to their presence. I also plead guilty to having committed breaches of on-the-water etiquette because of inattention.

With more and more people and an ever-expanding armada in our coastal waters, is there anything that serious fishermen can do other than take more blood-pressure medication? In spite of the frustration and anger that I have experienced and been witness to, I am convinced that for most anglers, and especially for fly rodders, there are workable solutions. Rules and regulations by authorities (e.g., no-wake zones), although helpful, have little to do with courtesy or respect for the rights of others. Courtesy cannot be legislated, but through education much can be done to improve the awareness and conduct of those using the water. Individual anglers and members of sportfishing clubs can make their concerns known to marina operators, boat dealers, tackle-shop proprietors, and restaurant owners. Fishermen are the bread and butter of many coastal businesses, especially during cooler seasons, when pleasure boaters stay at home and summer's sunbathers are long gone. I know of many marina operators and other business people who go out of their way to work with anglers. A discreet word of caution by a business owner to known offenders can bring about rapid reform. At some Jet Ski rental operations, customers are specifically asked to stay away from fishermen and fishing areas. Although there will always be a few jerks in every user group, most breaches of on-the-water etiquette are committed by people who just don't know any better. I have been impressed on several occasions by signs near boat ramps intended to educate the uninformed, and I believe that their use on a wider scale could have a positive impact. Printed reminders have included the following messages:

- Running through schools of fish puts them down for everyone!

- Whenever possible, avoid running near wading, drifting, or anchored fishermen.

- Don't crowd other anglers who arrived before you.

- When around fishermen, don't throw your anchor overboard . . . lower it.

Fly fishermen and anglers who anchor in heavily congested areas and in channels should not expect the world to stop or to revolve around them. Fishing in high-traffic areas is just asking for trouble. Fly fishermen should also not expect to be welcome where there is a concentration of jetty or surf fishermen, when fly lines and backcasts can create a nuisance.

Fly rodders can avoid many of the problems caused by overcrowding on the water if they change some of their own habits. Although much saltwater fly fishing is tide related, levels of light are also important. Early-morning outings are often the most productive and the most peaceful. In the first two hours of daylight I rarely see many boats, except for those of other serious anglers. Fishing in light rain and on gray, overcast days can also be excellent. Even night fly fishing, which has long been practiced in New England for weakfish and stripers, is beginning to catch on in other coastal areas.

Spring and fall water temperatures weed out many fair-weather boaters. From the Mid-Atlantic region south, and all along the Gulf states, there can be great fishing after Thanksgiving when weather conditions are right. In the sloughs of well-known bathing beaches, spotted weakfish and stripers may be the only swimmers in the early winter.

Many of the places that fly fishermen love are of little interest to trollers and bottom fishermen. Fly fishing is better adapted to shallow-water flats fishing than is any other kind of angling. The quiet preferred by fly fishermen is also contagious. Electric motors and even push poles used by fly rodders on flats are now being used by other light-tackle anglers. As indicated early in this book, fly fishermen can learn a lot from nonfly rodders. The irony is that anglers using spinning and conventional tackle are now learning about stealth and presentation from watching fly rodders.

Sport fishermen are an economic power in most coastal communities. The growing number of dedicated fly fishermen will increase that clout. The sportfishing community has the means to educate others about simple angling etiquette. There is no reason to suffer in silence. Letting operators of marinas and other coastal business owners know our concerns will be the quickest way to pass on the basics of etiquette to the fishing and nonfishing communities alike.

BOOKS MENTIONED IN
FLY FISHING THE TIDEWATERS

Bay, Kenneth E. *Salt Water Flies*. Philadelphia: J.P. Lippincott Co., 1972.

Kreh, Lefty. *Saltwater Fly Patterns*. New York: Lyons & Burford, Publishers, 1995.

————*Fly Fishing in Salt Water*. New York: Lyons & Burford, Publishers, 1986.

Sosin, Mark, and Kreh, Lefty. *Practical Fishing Knots*. New York: Lyons & Burford, Publishers, 1991.

Stewart, Dick and Farrow Allen. *Flies for Saltwater*. North Conway, NH: Mountain Pond Publishing, 1992.

Tabory, Lou. *Inshore Fly Fishing*. New York: Lyons & Burford, Publishers, 1992.

INDEX